COHESION
THE HUMAN ELEMENT IN COMBAT

COHESION
THE HUMAN ELEMENT IN COMBAT

Leadership and Societal Influence in the Armies of the Soviet Union, the United States, North Vietnam, and Israel

BY

Wm. Darryl Henderson

WITH AN INTRODUCTION BY

Charles C. Moskos

1985

NATIONAL DEFENSE

UNIVERSITY PRESS

WASHINGTON, DC

SSR, Inc., Washington, DC, furnished indexing services under contract DAHC32-85-M-1344.

Library of Congress Catalog Card Number: 84-601104

This book is for sale by the Superintendent of Documents, US Government Printing Office, Washington, DC 20402. Facsimile copies may be purchased from the following agencies: Registered users should contact the Defense Technical Information Center, Cameron Station, Alexandria, Virginia 22314. The general public should contact the National Technical Information Service, 5285 Port Royal Road, Springfield, Virginia 22161.

First printing, February 1985   Second printing, June 1986
Third printing, April 1989   Fourth printing, November 1993

In Memory of
Staff Sergeant Victor O. Fowler, Jr.
Company D, 5th Battalion, 7th Air Cavalry

CONTENTS

TABLES AND FIGURES

TABLE

FIGURE

FOREWORD

One of the perils for military planners in a high-tech world is to be taken in by the destructiveness of modern weapons and to give in to the currently popular theory that modern war will last for days or weeks rather than months or years—in short, to envision a world where technologies, not people, dominate war.

We can ill afford to dismiss the human element in combat. The stakes are far too great. Colonel Wm. Darryl Henderson, US Army, maintains that we cannot expect tactical situations in future fields of battle to be devoid of the human factor. Most recently, for example, Iraq's war with Iran was potentially a high-tech and swift war. That war is entering its fourth year and has cost, to date, 900,000 lives. Cohesion—mutual beliefs and needs that cause people to act as a collective whole—has so far played a more significant role in the Iran-Iraq war than all the sophisticated weapons on either side.

Does American society produce the type of soldier who would, under stress, suppress his individuality and act for the mutual good of the group? In the post-Vietnam, all-volunteer force environment, the kind of American citizen attracted to military service—the qualities he carries from society and what qualities the military organization is able to impart to him—must be a matter for serious thought and planning. Colonel Henderson's work is a step in that direction.

Richard D. Lawrence
Lieutenant General, US Army
President, National Defense University

ABOUT THE AUTHOR

COLONEL WM. DARRYL HENDERSON, US Army, wrote this book while attending the National War College where he was also a Senior Fellow at the National Defense University. He served earlier as a rifle platoon leader for two years and as a company commander for three years, including a tour in Vietnam as a company commander. He was seriously wounded by the North Koreans in the DMZ in 1975. Colonel Henderson also has served as a battalion commander and in the offices of the Secretary of Defense and the Chief of Staff of the Army. A combat veteran with a Ph.D. in Political Science, he has taught military psychology and international relations at West Point. Colonel Henderson is a coauthor of the *Handbook of World Conflict* and author of *Why the Vietcong Fought*.

PREFACE

IN ASSESSING WHO WINS WARS AND WHY, it is easy to overweigh any one factor and neglect others. Broad factors such as objectives and strategies, weapons and materials, technology, numbers of soldiers, and the human element must all be considered in determining who wins and why. Although this study is concerned with the human element in war, it recognizes the probability of major effects on war outcomes from other sources. Single-cause explanations must be avoided: they claim too much for one factor at the expense of others. This appears to be the case with today's emphasis on a defective US strategy as the prime explanation of the US loss in Vietnam and on technology as probably the determining factor in future modern wars. I want to register my reservations about three seemingly prevailing currents in contemporary thought about military affairs: the strategy-failure school explanation of the outcome in Vietnam; the high-technology school assertion that unit cohesion will not significantly affect future "high-tech" wars; and a related school assertion that cohesion can only be maintained in mass armies and not in small, specialized team armies of the future.

First, the Vietnam outcome: in a limited analysis of US strategy in Vietnam contrasting US strategy with the axioms of Clausewitz and the Principles of War, Colonel Harry G.

Summers, Jr., points to deficient US strategy as the main cause of the US loss in Vietnam.* This conclusion is probably not justified based on Colonel Summers' work. By limiting his analytical framework to Clausewitz and the Principles of War, Colonel Summers neglects a thorough examination of what many other knowledgeable observers have identified as the overall US strategy in Vietnam, that of "graduated compellance."

The chief objective of this strategy was to bring the North Vietnamese to the negotiating table on US terms through a process of escalating the costs of their involvement in the war. Because US strategy was determined primarily by civilian analysts, an examination of their product, its assumptions, and especially its underpinning in economic game theory in such books as Thomas Schelling's *Arms and Influence* and *The Strategy of Conflict* is essential. Further work must be done before the full story of US strategy in Vietnam is revealed. Perhaps an even more significant shortcoming of the strategy school is the failure to consider the quality of the human element on each side prior to determining reasons for the US defeat. The organization, policies, and leadership that created North Vietnamese Army resiliency to hardship, danger, and outside influences while their opponents were significantly affected by almost all elements within their environment are perhaps as important in explaining the final outcome of Vietnam as is defective US strategy.

In the future, the effect of high technology on military cohesion and combat effectiveness must be considered. The lethality and multiplier effects of new and modernized weapons systems will continue to modify the nature of war, as they have through history. From the time of the French Revolution and the beginning of the era of modern warfare, when French armies dominated the battlefield, cohesion and its relation to nationalism became a major factor in warfare. With major advances in the capabilities of wide numbers of weapons systems and accompanying operational doctrine, it has been suggested that the significance of military cohesion will decrease as a principal factor in determining the outcome of future battles, especially in the airland battles possible around the year 2000. The latest US Army

---

* Colonel Harry G. Summers, Jr., *On Strategy* (Novato, Calif.: Presidio, 1982).

field manual on this subject (FM 100-5) states that future major battles will likely be conducted within an integrated battlefield. This doctrine envisions the air-land battle to be characterized by deep attacks against follow-on echelons behind the front lines, principally through increased coordination of ground and air operations. The overall battlefield will be extended beyond the more traditional front lines and will encompass conventional, electronic, chemical, and possibly nuclear weapons, In viewing this future change in the characteristics of future battles, some observers have raised the important question of whether "by adapting military organization and tactics to the projected technology of the battlefield of the future, we run the risk of undermining the sources of social support that have historically sustained soldiers in battle."

Those who are most concerned with this possibility appear to be primarily influenced by the two major considerations.* One is the low personnel density in the form of relatively small weapons teams scattered widely over the battlefield because of weapon lethality, chemical contamination, and improved communications. The other consideration appears to be an implicit conclusion that cohesion that is congruent with Army objectives cannot exist without an undetermined but large number of troops organized into large maneuver elements that interact on a daily, face-to-face basis and thereby provide the social support necessary for cohesion. Others carry the argument further, stating that even if large armies were feasible, American society doesn't have the will to man such an army. Again technology is seen as the answer. Robert Cooper, Director of the Defense Advanced Research Projects Agency (DARPA), recently observed:

> It's my view that this society has decided that it will only use a certain fraction of its human effort in its own defense or in preparation for its own defense in peacetime. The imperative just isn't there. We are what we are. We don't have the resolve . . . so consequently we have no other alternative but to turn to high technology. That's it.**

---

* Unless otherwise indentified, the case for high technology has been taken from a widely circulated paper by David R. Segal, "Cohesion, Leadership and Stress in Airland Battle 2000," University of Maryland, 1983.

** See Michael Schrage, "The Sword of Science," *Washington Post Magazine,* 9 October 1983, pp. 22–23.

The counter proposition made here and in the chapters that follow is that cohesion will become even more important as the technology of war develops but that cohesion will probably also become more difficult to achieve. The chance, dispersion, isolation, confusion, danger, stress, and hardship of the future battlefield will ensure that the decades-old trend of authority and decisionmaking moving downward in the organization will continue. A form of warfare where soldiers marched lock-step into battle in long lines under the watchful eye of a sergeant behind them with drawn sword has changed to one of the small, independent-unit tactics and leadership found in recent wars. Perhaps the 1973 Arab-Israeli war best illustrates this trend. The 1973 war was the largest tank battle ever fought, yet it was characterized by numerous small unit engagements most often won by the side displaying the most initiative, leadership, and cohesion at the small-unit level.

Statements and research findings that support the view that cohesion will be less important in future small and more specialized armies appear to be unduly dependent upon study of the American Army, especially in Korea and Vietnam, and lead to the tentative conclusion that research has not shed any light on the critical social mass or size of group necessary to provide cohesion in military units. However, research is available (for example, on Israeli, Chinese, and North Vietnamese armies) that suggests that strong military cohesion is possible in quite small groups and under intense pressure and stress. In fact, in both the Chinese and North Vietnamese examples, three-man military cells are used as the basic building block in constructing cohesive units following their 3 x 3 organizational concept. In it, each unit is one of three like units which are part of a larger unit also comprised of three like units. In both armies, the central focus of cohesion is at the very small unit level. The three-man military cell with proper leadership and control became the strength upon which the extraordinary endurance of both armies was based. This is especially significant in the case of the North Vietnamese Army (NVA) since it was required to operate widely dispersed under the conditions of extreme hardship and stress often described as characteristic of future battlefields. In this regard, it is also interesting to note how the Israeli Army deals with battle stress similar to the type envisioned in future wars. During the 1973 and Lebanon conflicts, treatment of stress casualties had the goal of returning the soldier to duty with his unit. The power and attraction of the small cohesive unit to the soldier helped achieve a remarkably high rate of success in treating his battle stress.

It has also been suggested that the importance of cohesion in explaining combat performance has been overstated or that cohesion can be replaced by alternative sources of motivation and control (from patriotism to drugs). Support for the view that the significance of cohesion has been overstated is made by some who point to prior studies describing soldiers who fought as individuals rather than as part of a cohesive unit. Such conclusions are probably questionable. Although in some instances US soldiers might have fought as individuals in Vietnam, no one, to my knowledge, has seriously proposed this form of combat motivation as a superior one.*

Related suggestions also discount military cohesion by suggesting that patriotism can be an alternative combat motivator. The view of cohesion as an isolated phenomenon on the battlefield indicates a narrow comprehension of the nature of military cohesion and its origins. It is important to recognize the various sources of cohesion. Patriotism or nationalism are not alternative motivators; rather, they manifest themselves in cohesive units by helping provide the well-integrated group values and communications necessary for military cohesion.

Another suggestion, that smarter soldiers require less of the social support and leadership that bind cohesive units together, appears to be made upon an incomplete examination of the evidence. Those armies that have enjoyed the highest degrees of cohesion and combat effectiveness in the past have achieved such success in part because they relied upon the most qualified and the smartest people available (for example, the Israeli and NVA Armies). Certainly, an army that has the smartest people available in its ranks has greater capability. It also has a far greater

---

* The primary research in this area is descriptive, not prescriptive, and should not be interpreted that combat motivation based on individual survival is a superior form of combat motivation. See Charles C. Moskos, "The American Combat Soldier in Vietnam," *Journal of Social Issues* 31 (1975): 27.

challenge in motivating and leading more active, intellectually diverse, and questioning soldiers.

Still others, apparently generalizing on the American experience in Vietnam, have suggested that because of the socialization of American youth, today's US soldier now requires less social support of the type traditionally found in cohesive units. But one is reminded that the Principles of War, which apply equally to all nations, are autonomous and that an army that achieves the greatest cohesion will win, everything else being equal. One cannot view American society and its impact on the US Army in isolation. The US Army must be capable of competing with other armies. Accommodations with the "dictates" of American society and domestic politics must also be considered in view of the Army's mission. The Arab-Israeli wars illustrate this point well. The cohesion and leadership evident in Israeli society and in the Israeli Army are described in later chapters. Contrast with this the Arab soldier who does not benefit from a strong socialization process emphasizing strong loyalties and social ties beyond the family. The result is the weak leadership and noncohesive practices of many Arab armies. Hence, the Arab soldier, although he may be well trained, often becomes an isolated and lonely individual in the face of stress and danger on the battlefield. As described in a following chapter, this has been a major factor in the many Israeli victories in the Middle East.

Finally, the suggestion that drugs be seriously considered as an alternative form of motivation in view of the expected loss of social support on the modern battlefield is very questionable. Numerous moral, physiological, and other questions can be imagined.

A common thread that appears in each of the above suggestions is their basis in the American experience and in the future impact of high technology on the battlefield. The danger is that other armies have dealt with the problems raised here far more effectively and appear to offer a more proven basis for generalizing about the future of cohesion on the modern battlefield. In this regard, it seems certain that the army that succeeds in creating and maintaining cohesive units on future battlefields will have a significant advantage over those that do not.

ACKNOWLEDGMENTS

I WISH TO GRATEFULLY RECOGNIZE Morris Janowitz, University of Chicago, Charles Moskos, Northwestern University, and Fred Kiley, National Defense University, for very generously providing assistance to me in writing this book. Their reviews of the draft manuscript and comments were especially valued.

Other friends and professional associates also assisted with suggestions and were especially encouraging with their comments. John Johns, Wes Clark, Robert Berls, William Odem, Don Anderson, and Ruevan Gal, former chief psychologist of the Israeli Defense Forces, deserve special acknowledgment.

Several other individuals within the Research Directorate must also be recognized for their assistance: George Maerz, senior editor, Rebecca Miller, editor, and Carol Valentine, editorial typist, who spent many hours on my manuscript.

WM. DARRYL HENDERSON

INTRODUCTION

BY *Charles C. Moskos*

THAT MEN too often find themselves fighting wars is a depressing commentary on both history and contemporary life. That many of these same men endure situations where they can be killed or kill others is a perplexing fact of human behavior. It is not surprising, then, that interpretations of the motivations of men in combat are many and that the library on the subject is voluminous. *Cohesion: The Human Element in Combat* by Wm. Darryl Henderson says something, however, that is both new and important; at the same time it restates verities that are old and yet have to be rediscovered.

Colonel Henderson brings to this book a unique set of credentials. He commanded a rifle company in Vietnam during 1966–67, and suffered a near mortal personal attack by North Koreans on the Demilitarized Zone in 1975. But Colonel Henderson brings more than direct combat experience to this study. He holds a Ph.D. in comparative and international politics and is the author of *Why the Vietcong Fought* (1979), a detailed, provocative, and convincing study of one of the most effective armies of modern times.

Cohesion: The Human Element in Combat is even more ambitious because it uses the most difficult of all research methodologies—the comparative approach. It is comparative in several ways. We are presented with information and analyses on four quite different armies, those of the United States, Israel, North Vietnam, and the Soviet Union. The reader is introduced to basic variables relating to the human element in combat, which in turn are applied and compared with each other within each of the four countries. Henderson has defined the following as key variables: the military unit's ability to provide for the soldier's main needs, unit integrity and stability, the soldier's perception of escaping the unit, unit motivation and control, deviance from unit norms, commonality of values, factors promoting small-unit cohesion, and leadership in cohesive units. It is the comparative mode of analysis and the clear specification of variables which give this study of unit cohesion its unique and most valuable quality.

At the outset, it must be noted that *Cohesion: The Human Element in Combat* sets itself apart from the prevailing viewpoints on combat motivations and the dominant tendencies in military manpower policy. By making unit cohesion the focus of the study, Colonel Henderson gives little support to those who see advancing military technology revolutionizing warfare to the extent that the social psychological processes of small groups of men in tactical situations are, at best, secondary considerations. Unlike too many others, Colonel Henderson regards the impending disappearance of the ground combat soldier in modern warfare to be greatly exaggerated.

Cohesion: The Human Element in Combat also runs counter to the prevalent notion that military leadership per se, with its implied convictions that "can-doism" can overcome deficiencies in soldiers and organization, is the salient feature of small-unit performance. By pointing to the systemic factors affecting combat performance, Colonel Henderson points to the limits of leadership as an explanatory factor in differential combat outcomes.

This book is also to be contrasted with the school of thought that holds that erroneous strategic formulations were the principal cause of the American failure in Vietnam. Colonel Henderson provides a corrective to this viewpoint by his reemphasis on the centrality of cohesion in small units and the tactical nature of warfare.

Cohesion: The Human Element in Combat must also be placed in the context of theoretical studies of military sociology. Broadly speaking, studies of armed forces and society usually proceed along one or the other of two levels of analyses. On the one hand, the analysis focuses on the societal, cultural, and political context of military systems; on the other, the emphasis is on the internal organization of the military system. Whether or not one views the armed forces as an independent or dependent variable shapes policy conclusions as well. The issue can be posed as to which matters more, the qualities the soldier brings into the military or what happens to the soldier once he is in the military. What distinguishes Colonel Henderson's study is that it gives due attention to both factors—and does so for four different armies. The military is not treated in isolation from the societal context and the values soldiers bring with them; at the same time, the unique and specific qualities of the military organization and, above all, of the combat situation are clearly kept in focus. Colonel Henderson bridges the gap between the level of microanalysis based on individual behavior and the level of macroanalysis based on variables common to sociology.

Finally, and most important, Henderson sets himself against those who view the military in system analyses and econometric terms. The importance of systems analysts in public counsel is not, of course, a recent innovation, but what is new is the effort to apply system analyses to issues of combat performance. This implies a redefinition of military service away from an institutional format to one more and more resembling that of an occupation.

Such a redefinition of military service is based on a set of core assumptions. First, there is no analytical distinction between military and other systems—in particular, no difference between cost-effectiveness analysis of civilian enterprises and military services. Second, that military compensation should as much as possible be in cash, rather than in kind or deferred, thereby allowing for a more efficient operation of the marketplace. By 1983, a private first class was earning about $15,000 a year if he lived (as was becoming more common) off base. And, third, that unit cohesion and goal commitment are essentially unmeasurable, therefore an inappropriate object of analyses. Colonel Henderson's study counters each of these assumptions.

The most subtle point of Colonel Henderson's study is that he has taken the small unit as the object of analysis. We constantly forget that combat behavior (as is true for most human behavior) must be understood in the context of the small group in which individuals operate. While it is much easier to measure individual aptitudes and attributes, the central point is that social psychological, rather than psychologistic, variables are most salient. This has been a hard lesson to absorb in the military social science community.

I wish I could say that I am sure that the lessons of this book will be absorbed by the world of military consultants and those responsible for manpower policy at the highest levels. Yet, I fear, even though *Cohesion: The Human Element in Combat* offers a sophisticated comparative methodology, the quantifiers of the manpower establishment in the Department of Defense will not be impressed. This is sad for both the country and its soldiers. Because the methods used in this book are holistic, qualitative, and comparative, they will probably be slighted by those seeking so-called "hard data." The pseudo-quantification reflected in the marketplace approach to military manpower will most likely continue to ascend. Yet, in the long run, by attaching a market value to military service, econometricians and the manpower establishment of the Department of Defense have cheapened, rather than enhanced, the value many soldiers and many Americans believed it had.

Cohesion: The Human Element in Combat is written at a time when the American Army is seeking to recover an internal balance it lost both in the Vietnam war and in the early years of the all-volunteer force. At the time this book was going to press, the American public was being told that the Army had turned the corner. Certainly there was reason for cautious optimism in light of an upturn in recruit quality, more rigorous training procedures, and Army initiatives to enhance unit cohesion. Yet there was a kind of Pollyannaish glow to the reports on the improved Army.

Long-term and systemic factors contributing to diminished combat effectiveness were still operative. That Colonel Henderson addresses these issues frontally means he goes against the grain. He brings clarity to what are literally life-and-death matters.

September 1983

CHAPTER I

The Significance of Military Cohesion

BY ALL TRADITIONAL METHODS of measuring military power, the United States and its allied forces should have had little difficulty defeating the North Vietnamese during the second Vietnamese war (1965–1972). At the height of its involvement in Vietnam, the United States was spending in excess of $25 billion a year. The US Army had committed 40 percent of all its combat-ready divisions. They were supported by 50 percent of US tactical air power and one-third of US Naval Forces.[1] Combined with allied contributions, US forces overwhelmed the North Vietnamese numerically in all traditional categories of military power.

In opposition, the North Vietnamese fielded an army in the south that was inferior in strength and significantly inferior in logistical support, firepower, and mobility.[2] Never before had such massive firepower been concentrated against an opposing army in such a limited area for such an extended period of time. In view of the overwhelming military power opposing it, North Vietnam had to rely on the human factor. Van Tien Dung, Army Chief of Staff, outlined their strategy:

> Our arms and equipment were weaker than the enemy's thus we could only develop moral superiority (within the army)

1

and only then have the courage to attack the enemy, only then
dare to fight the enemy resolutely, only then could we stand
solidly before all difficult trials created by the superior firepower that the enemy had brought into the war.[3]

Following this strategy, the North Vietnamese Army maintained
its cohesion and endured while all other armies were defeated or
retired from the battlefield.

With some validity, conventional wisdom in the United
States attributes the North Vietnamese "victory" to the rapid decline in public support for the US war effort after the Tet Offensive in 1968. The US public determined that further efforts were
not worth the costs. This change in public attitude soon transferred into policy and the United States withdrew.

This, of course, is only a partial explanation. Another part
involves how the North Vietnamese Army endured the most
concentrated firepower ever directed against an army for seven
continuous years. When Van Tien Dung spoke of "moral
superiority" within the ranks of the North Vietnamese Army, he
was referring to what many analysts consider the creation of one
of the most cohesive armies ever fielded. The attention paid within that army to organization, leadership, care of the soldier, and
development of military cohesion and psychological control within the smallest units has not been equalled by other modern
armies.[4] The North Vietnamese Army was able to endure some of
the greatest stress of combat and hardship because of its extensive
development of the human element.[5]

Remarkable as it may seem, the North Vietnamese experience
is not unique. Strategists such as Clausewitz, Napoleon, and Mao
Tse Tung preceded Ho Chi Minh in recognizing the effect and importance of the human element in warfare. Examples can be cited
from the Punic Wars through World War II, the Korean war, and
the Vietnam war. Unfortunately, in most cases all that was noted
were interesting stories implying the importance of the cohesion,
but little was said about how this cohesion was created or maintained.

A similar situation occurred most recently in the Falklands
war. During the weeks it took the British Fleet to steam to the occupied Falkland Islands, analysts throughout the world assessed
the opposing forces. Conclusions on the probable outcome were

made on the basis of opposing numbers and technical capabilities, which were known with reasonable accuracy. Opposing numbers of troops were weighed. The advantage of shoreline defense versus amphibious landings and the capabilities of the limited numbers of British Harriers versus more numerous Argentine A-4 Skyhawks and Mirages were considered. The relative strength of the naval forces involved and the enormous difficulties for the British in mounting a major naval and amphibious operation at the end of an extremely long sea line of communication were discussed at length. Even the weather of the approaching winter in the southern hemisphere was considered in pronouncements about possible outcomes. Such assessments were further favored by the isolation of the theater and the apparent nature of the key terrain. Almost every significant factor was considered except the one that was to become the most important, the human element.[6] The opposing qualities of the individual soldiers and their organization, leadership, and cohesion became the deciding factor in the war. In battle, it became apparent that the Argentine Army was decisively outclassed. Although they outnumbered the British and although their weapons and supplies were more than adequate, it became clear that the Argentines lacked the will to prevail that is characteristic in cohesive, well-led units. This became even more apparent when, during negotiations for surrender, a main Argentine condition was that their officers be allowed to retain their side arms for protection against their own men.

Measuring Military Power

The failure to consider the human element in war adequately and an overemphasis on weapon capabilities, numbers of troops, and other concrete factors are caused by the difficulty in quantifying the human element, whereas the more tangible factors are easily counted, totaled, and compared.[7]

The preparation for and the analysis of modern warfare are traditionally divided into four broad elements: (1) strategy, (2) weapons and materiel, (3) technology, and (4) numbers of soldiers. Seldom is there any analysis of the human element.

The Human Element

The human element has been referred to in such terms as esprit de corps, group morale, and elan. Various analysts have emphasized these terms differently, but they have all tended to refer to the motivation of the individual soldier as part of a group. Currently, the favored term, *cohesion*, is given a broader and more definitive meaning. Recognizing that small-group norms can militate against the organization, some writers prefer to use the term "military cohesion" to signify that small-unit norms are in congruence with army objectives and goals. More specifically, cohesion has been defined as

> the bonding together of members of an organization/unit in such a way as to sustain their will and commitment to each other, their unit, and the mission.[8]

Even more specifically, cohesion exists in a unit when the primary day-to-day goals of the individual soldier, of the small group with which he identifies, and of unit leaders are congruent—with each giving his primary loyalty to the group so that it trains and fights as a unit with all members willing to risk death to achieve a common objective.[9]

Cohesion, as described above, is the determining factor in assessing and comparing the human element of opposing armies. The nature of modern war indicates that small-unit cohesion is the only force capable of causing soldiers to expose themselves consistently to enemy fire in pursuit of an army's goals. The confusion, danger, hardship, and isolation of the modern battlefield have caused a pronounced de-emphasis on strict orders, rote training, and coercive discipline. At the same time, there has been a significant shift downward in the control of soldiers in combat. Accompanying these changes has been increased emphasis on controlling soldiers through an internalization of values and operating rules congruent with the objectives, goals, and values of the organization. The need for these changes has been recognized to some degree within most armies but especially by the Vietnamese and the Chinese. Early in the organization of their armies, they realized their need to rely on the human element in view of their inferiority in weapons and technology. Mao preached:

> In all armies, obedience of the subordinates to their superiors must be exacted . . . but the basis for soldier discipline must be the individual conscience. With soldiers, a discipline of coercion is ineffective, discipline must be self-imposed, because only when it is, is the soldier able to understand

completely why he fights and how he must obey. This type of discipline becomes a tower of strength within the army, and it is the only type that can truly harmonize the relationship that exists between officers and soldiers.[10]

Why Soldiers Fight

Mao recognized that in modern war the individual soldier is alone except for two or three close comrades on his right and left. The formal organization of the army has no means even to keep the soldier in view, much less closely supervise his behavior. For this reason, the significance of the small unit to which the soldier belongs can hardly be overstated. The small group develops strong rules of behavior and expectations about individual conduct on the basis of face-to-face relationships and thereby becomes the immediate determinant of the soldier's behavior. In a unit that is properly led and controlled by its leaders, all other influences become secondary. Such overwhelming influence of the small group in war as well as peace has been documented in many armies.[11] Shils and Janowitz, for example, quote a World War II German soldier who makes the point clearly:

> The company is the only truly existent community. This community allows neither time nor rest for a personal life. It forces us into its circle, for life is at stake. Obviously, compromises must be made and claims surrendered. Therefore the idea of fighting, living, and dying for the fatherland is but a relatively distant thought. At least it does not play a great role in the practical motivation of the individual.[12]

Describing the actions of soldiers in Korea, Alexander George makes essentially the same case:

> The most significant persons for the combat soldier are the men who fight by his side and share with him the ordeal of trying to survive.[13]

And S.L.A. Marshall, who has observed soldiers in numerous wars and armies, observes:

> I hold it to be one of the simplest truths of war that the thing which enables an infantry soldier to keep going with his weapons is the near presence or the presumed presence of a comrade.[14]

Well-written fiction also recognizes this basic truth about war.[15] In *All Quiet on the Western Front*, Erich Remarque speaks of the importance of the soldier's comrades:

> These voices, these quiet words, these footsteps in trench behind me recall me at a bound from the terrible loneliness and fear of death by which I had been almost destroyed. They are more to me than life, those voices, they are more than motherliness and more than fear; they are the strongest, most comforting thing there is anywhere, they are the voices of my comrades.[16]

Several wars and over 50 years later, James Webb writes in *Fields of Fire* of the Vietnam soldier's link with his fellows:

> The bald, red hills with their sandbag bunkers, the banter and frolic of dirt-covered grunts, the fearful intensity of contact. . . . Down south his men were on patrol, or digging new perimeters, or dying, and he was nothing if he did not share that misery.[17]

Methodology

The impact of the primary group on unit cohesion is recognized by all observers as very significant (see appendix). Even those who suggest it has limitations agree that the concept of the primary group is central in explaining a soldier's behavior.[18] Most of the discussion concerning the degree to which the primary group should be credited for explaining why men fight, however, appears to be of the straw-man variety. Social scientists generally do not attribute the soldier's willingness to fight solely to the primary group. All recognize that primary group influences can militate against organizational goals unless appointed leaders become the dominant influence within the group. Furthermore, Janowitz, one of the earliest analysts to recognize the importance of the primary group in explaining a soldier's behavior, states that the concept of the primary group must be included within a "theory of organizational behavior in which an array of sociological concepts is employed." [19]

In a recent effort to describe the soldier's motivation, Anthony Kellet states that an approach "combining individual, organizational, and social factors with situational ones offers a more complete explanation of combat motivation." [20]

Purpose

The purpose of this study is to offer an approach for assessing and comparing cohesion among armies. This approach centers on the influence of the small group on the soldier's daily life but also takes into account organizational, situational, and social factors such as leadership, socialization, ideology, organizational support and policies, and the stress caused by combat and hardship. The appropriate focus of such an approach is on the small unit because this is the only locus within an army where the individual soldier with his personal characteristics, influenced by his socialization and ideology, can be observed within the organization. Together with the small group facing situational factors, the organization is also very visible at this level with its leadership, policies, and support.

Research Plan

The comparative method is used to contrast and measure indicators of cohesion in four armies. These indicators are drawn from an ideal model of a cohesive unit presented in chapters 2 and 3. Chapters 5 and 7 outline broad societal and leadership factors that influence the soldier within his small group, factors which, in turn, affect cohesion. Each of these conceptual chapters is then used in the succeeding chapters as the basis for contrasting and assessing the degree of cohesion in different armies. Existing contrasts in different areas affecting cohesion are illustrated by the use of charts with arbitrary weightings designed to highlight the contrasts described in the text. These, of course, are not definitive but depend upon the judgment of the analyst. Chapter 9 presents conclusions and recommendations.

A basic premise of this study is that it is possible and very useful to synthesize secondary knowledge and conclusions from a variety of sources and disciplines that have already been developed and are widely acknowledged. Although my primary research into the combat motivation of the North Vietnamese soldier has had a significant influence on my approach,[21] I have also relied on many other sources.[22]

Finally, this effort is not limited to cohesion in Western armies or in armies from developed countries, but relies on knowledge and findings on cohesion and combat motivation in armies worldwide. Investigation of cohesion limited to Western democracies significantly constrains the examination and ultimately limits the understanding of cohesion and combat motivation.[23] Perhaps even more significant is the possible danger of generalizing about the military power of a potential non-democratic opponent that has a highly developed system for promoting cohesion—solely on the basis of knowledge gained from examining motivation in Western armies.

It is a mistake to assume that a democracy or any other type of government is guaranteed an army inherently better than that of neighboring political systems. This is especially true of democracies that have forgotten that personal and individual sacrifices are necessary to build an army sufficient for their protection—those in which the citizens have become increasingly self-indulgent, lacking the self-discipline and sense of responsibility necessary to assume their share of the common defense while missing few opportunities to assert their rights.

CHAPTER II

Characteristics of a Cohesive Army

EVIDENCE OF COHESION in an army must be sought where it occurs—at the small-unit level among the intimate, face-to-face groups that emerge in peacetime as well as in war. As already defined, military cohesion involves the bonding of members of a unit in such a way as to sustain their will and commitment to each other, the organization, and the mission.[1] In view of the general consensus of what a cohesive army is, any ordering of characteristics of such an army must consider the following areas: the overall organizational structure, which includes the party, army, or other sources of goals, policy, and support; the "human element" or the small intimate groups that control and motivate soldiers through their norms; and the influence of the leader on the small group and the resulting commitment of the individual soldier toward achieving army goals.

The only level in an army where these three factors simultaneously occur—and therefore the most appropriate focus of research on cohesion—is that point at which the organization, the small group, and the leader come together in an army: the lower levels of the organization. Squad, platoon, and section-level units are ideal for this approach because the formal organization is evident at this level, because it is possible to observe how small-group

9

members respond as individuals within these organizations, and because leadership techniques and their impact on the small group are also visible at this level.

Organizational Characteristics

Perhaps the primary function of the organization is to provide purpose to the cohesive unit in the form of goals and objectives. If the purpose of war is the achievement of political ends, then the overall organization of an army must serve to transmit these political goals through a "chain of command" to those specific units ultimately charged with accomplishing the goals.[2] In this way, the broad, political purposes of a party or a nation penetrate the small cohesive group.

Another function of organizational top management is to provide the varied support required by lower-level cohesive units. Personnel and logistical support, as well as policies designed to promote cohesion, is required of the organization and is discussed in detail in the next chapter.

A final function of the organization is to prescribe structural characteristics for the small unit that will promote cohesion. The purpose of these structural characteristics is to de-emphasize individualism within the soldier. Instead, the small unit is structured to promote responsibility. The soldier is constantly reminded of his responsibilities to his buddies, to his leaders, to the squad, to the platoon, and ultimately to the people and the nation or party through the structure of his immediate unit.

Certain organizational characteristics are thus important: the size of the group, for example, takes on added significance, because cohesion is inversely proportional to the numbers in the group. Several armies, in fact, have determined that the ideal size is up to nine men, with some armies choosing a three-man unit or military cell, which becomes the basic personnel building block of the army. Another factor is the soldier's belief about the duration of his commitment to the unit. Cohesion is promoted the longer the soldier anticipates remaining in his unit. And the frequency with which soldiers associate with each other is also important. The greater the frequency of association in pursuit of common purposes, the greater the cohesion. Finally, the more fully structured the associations among soldiers within the group become, the more influence the unit will have over the soldiers. Structured associations also serve to establish boundaries around the group and form a clear distinction between members and nonmembers, or between "us" and "them." [3]

Small Group and Unit Characteristics

Small, cohesive units usually have several discernible characteristics. The unit serves as a basic, tactical, fire-and-maneuver or service unit. The cohesive unit must function as a "buddy group" capable of satisfying basic physiological and social needs for the individual soldier. Another characteristic is the presence of a dominant group, which controls the day-to-day behavior of the soldier. The leader operates within this group to ensure that group norms or expectations of behavior are congruent with organizational objectives. A final characteristic is the existence of an observation-and-reporting system that is self-correcting for deviance from group norms by mobilizing peer groups or leadership pressures in order to correct individual behavior.

Leadership Characteristics

Leadership is the most important factor in achieving congruence between unit norms and organizational objectives. For leaders to be effective in influencing the emergence of norms compatible with organizational objectives, leadership must be based upon personal relationships between leaders and soldiers, rather than upon an impersonal managerial style.[4] Specific functions characterize effective leadership in a cohesive unit. The leader must transmit organizational goals or objectives effectively from the chain of command to the small, cohesive group. Then he must lead the unit in achieving these objectives through his personal influence and technical expertise. The leader must also maintain unit cohesion by ensuring continuous organizational support and by the detection and correction of deviance from group norms. Finally, the leader assists in making or maintaining an ideologically-sound soldier by setting an example, by teaching, and by indoctrinating.

Because the organization, the individual soldier, and the leader all come together in the small unit, this level is best suited for investigating the degree of cohesion in an army. Small, cohesive units are characterized by specific functions. To summarize:

1. Functions of the larger organization are to
    a. establish goals and objectives;
    b. provide support;
    c. prescribe small-unit policies for
        (1) numbers (cohesion is inverse to size);
        (2) duration (the longer, the stronger cohesion becomes);
        (3) frequency (the more association, the more cohesion is promoted);
        (4) structure (the more structured the relationships, the more cohesion is promoted).
2. Functions of the small unit are to
    a. serve as a "buddy group" satisfying basic needs of the soldier;
    b. serve as a dominant group controlling behavior of soldiers, within which the leader acts to ensure group norms are congruent with organizational objectives;
    c. provide a mutual observation and reporting system that mobilizes peer and leader pressures to correct individual deviance;
    d. serve as a basic, tactical, fire-and-maneuver or operational unit.
3. Functions of the leader are to
    a. transmit organization goals to the small group;
    b. lead the unit in achieving goals;
    c. maintain desired small-group norms by ensuring organizational support and detection and correction of deviance;
    d. create or maintain an ideologically sound soldier through setting example, teaching, or indoctrination.

CHAPTER III

Assessing Cohesion in Small Units

SMALL-UNIT COHESION capable of causing soldiers to expose themselves to enemy fire in pursuit of unit objectives must also satisfy certain needs for the soldier. Individual soldiers must identify with their immediate unit leaders, and the unit must satisfy physical, security, and social needs. The cohesive unit becomes, in effect, a social and support organization capable of satisfying the soldier's major needs.

Physical, Security, and Social Needs

A soldier will not willingly stay in a unit unless physical, security, and social needs are met. Most armies are able to meet them to some degree, but many have difficulty in the confusion and displacement of war. A cohesive unit will provide adequate food, water, medical support, and essential supplies and weapons at all times but will also endure during periods of scarcity when other less cohesive units would disintegrate. For a unit to endure, it must receive logistical support that, in the eyes of unit members, will allow the unit to survive the situation faced by the unit.

13

Whether the small unit is the dominant primary group for the individual soldier is of the utmost importance. Primary social affiliation within the unit is an extremely significant indicator of cohesion because it means that the small military unit has replaced other influences such as the family as the primary determinant of the soldier's day-to-day behavior. In such a unit, the soldier becomes bound by the expectations and needs of his fellow soldiers. Such relationships completely overshadow other obligations and claims on his loyalties. It is not necessary that the primacy of the unit be formally recognized. The soldier merely recognizes that more immediate considerations and relationships have displaced family, parents, and friends as the prime determinant of his behavior. Despite the intensity of the relationship, it is not usually seen as permanent but as one that is limited to a specific period or to the duration of the conflict.

Such devotion to a cohesive unit does not, of course, occur spontaneously. Besides reliable logistical support, a cohesive unit provides the major source of esteem and recognition for unit members. Because a unit is able to meet this powerful need, the soldier tends to dedicate his time and energy to it, to its activities, and to its goals. Conversely, in units where these needs are not met, the soldier will seek them outside the unit, and often in groups with goals not congruent with those of the army. Leaders need to plan and create these conditions for cohesion systematically.

The cohesive unit also requires an environment that promotes a strong sense of mutual affection among unit members. The greater the degree of challenge, hardship, and danger, the greater the development of mutual affection and attraction among unit members. Such attraction can occur in peace as well as in combat. For a purpose to be perceived as worthwhile by the group, what seems to be necessary is common exposure to hardship, or to difficult training, or to danger. Of course, the role of the leader in establishing the goals and in leading the formation of the unit members' opinion about the significance of those goals is paramount.

Preventing the soldiers' alienation not only from the group but also from the unit's leaders is a responsibility of leadership. The soldier will tend to identify strongly with his unit and its leaders if the leader conducts his relationships with his subordinates in a manner that convinces the soldier that influence is a two-way street and that he, the soldier, is not merely at the end of a long, impersonal chain of command. Instead, the leader must ensure that the soldier does not become alienated and that he obtains a sense of influence over some of the events that occur in his immediate unit. Those events include passes, chow, safety measures, or other unit activities controlled by his immediate leaders.

Events outside the control of immediate unit leaders can also contribute to the soldier's identification with his unit. Cohesion occurs when the unit and its leaders act to protect the soldier from and to regulate relations with higher authorities. An example involves the situation when soldiers perceive orders or allocations from higher headquarters as being unfair or inadequate. The sergeant, platoon leader, or company commander who goes to higher headquarters and wins relief or who merely makes the attempt not only increases his influence among his soldiers but also significantly contributes to their sense of belonging to a group that can deal with an otherwise uncaring environment. What is important in such situations is not whether the leader was able to correct the perceived inequity but that the leader's foremost priority was the unit. Also important is the unit members' perception that, whatever the outcome, they and their leaders will share its effects equally and that the unit is a vehicle through which the individual is taken care of.

Although small-group cohesion can exist independently of unit leaders, unit cohesion that accepts and reinforces army goals and purposes as the unit's own can only occur consistently when soldiers identify closely with their immediate leaders.

In summary, the soldier identifies strongly with his unit when the unit satisfies his major physical, security, and social needs. A cohesive unit
1. provides adequate food, water, medical support, rest, and essential supplies and weapons;
2. is the primary social group for the individual soldier and controls his day-to-day behavior;

3. provides the major source of esteem and recognition;
4. provides a strong sense of mutual affection and attraction among unit members;
5. protects the soldier from and regulates relations with higher authorities;
6. provides the soldier a sense of influence over events in his immediate unit; and
7. causes the soldier to identify strongly with immediate unit leaders at squad, section, platoon, and company levels.

A Soldier's Perception of Successfully Escaping the Unit

The soldier's perception of his chances to avoid service or escape his unit successfully for the civilian world significantly affects unit cohesion. There must be no conflict within the soldier's mind concerning his personal reasons for remaining with his unit. He must perceive no option other than service with his unit. When the soldier thinks beyond his buddies and the group, he must be able to justify to himself, with minimum doubt, why he chooses to endure hardship and danger with his unit when a familiar civilian environment, offering comfort and safety, is nearby. If soldiers perceive that relatively harmless administrative avenues of escape are open, or if soldiers believe the penalties for desertion are relatively light, cohesion in a unit will be weakened. If such courses are clouded with ambiguity, however, and the soldier has significant doubts about his ability to leave his unit successfully, he will conclude that he is committed for the duration and will see his best chances for survival as dependent upon the members of his immediate unit.

To achieve this end, a cohesive unit will ensure that the soldier is aware of all legal, moral, and physical barriers that separate him from the civilian world and bind him to his unit. As a result, the ambiguous and often alien nature of the world beyond the borders of the unit should be emphasized, especially to young soldiers.

Other factors supporting cohesion are linked directly to broad, societal agreement about the citizen's duty to serve in defense of the nation and indirectly to the nation's potential for nationalism. Soldiers must be aware that their society will exact significant penalties for being AWOL and for deserting and will attach significant social sanctions for "bad paper" discharges. The soldier must also perceive that chances for avoiding such punishment are small for those who choose to avoid service. There can be no expectation that sanctions and penalties will be lifted or eased at a later date or that those who avoided service will be valued equally with those who served.

Cohesive units will also benefit from internal army policies that do not grant administrative and medical discharges or transfers easily. Another significant set of policies concerns the provisions made by the society to recognize successful completion of a soldier's tour of service. Tangible and significant rewards such as job preference, assistance with education (such as the GI Bill) or assistance in purchasing property (with VA loans) are examples of a society's recognizing the sacrifices soldiers endure. The greater the emphasis on these rewards, the greater the attraction of military service and the stronger the bonding of a soldier to his unit.

In sum, if unit policy and societal norms cause the soldier to perceive that all courses for leaving his unit are problematical while positive group and societal practices attract him toward his group, then unit cohesion will be strengthened. A cohesive unit

1. will ensure that the soldier is aware of all legal, moral, and physical barriers that separate him from the remainder of society and that tend to keep him within his unit;
2. will not grant discharges and transfers easily;
3. will attach significant social sanctions for "bad paper" discharges;
4. will exact significant penalties for being AWOL and for deserting; and
5. will recognize and reward successful completion of tours of service.

Maintenance of Unit Integrity and Stability

The soldier will identify more closely with his unit, and cohesion will be strengthened, if organizational policies give priority to maintaining unit integrity during off-duty and maintenance hours as well as during training and operations. Personnel policies, to include replacement practices, should also emphasize maintenance of unit integrity.

Creating and maintaining cohesion requires a firm policy of relying on small-unit rotation, rather than on individual replacements, as well as an emphasis on personnel stability within units. From a management perspective, it is often much more efficient to assign individual replacements, based upon skills and the needs of the army. However, treating individual soldiers as "spare parts" in a large and complex personnel machine fails to recognize why men fight in combat. Cohesion, that state binding men together as members of a combat unit capable of enduring the stress of danger and hardship, is dependent upon personnel stability within small units.

The creation of a cohesive unit is best accomplished upon its initial formation, before other norms form that are incongruent with army values. Creating a cohesive unit requires an intensive resocialization process. The determinants of the new recruit's day-to-day behavior must be replaced by a new set of rules based on his perceptions of what his new fellow soldiers and his leaders expect. This type of resocialization is best created through a rites-of-passage process that totally consumes the soldier's attention and efforts for an extended period and from which he emerges with a new or adapted set of operating rules for his daily life. These norms must be firmly grounded in the bonds and expectations formed between him, his fellow soldiers, and his immediate leaders. It must be emphasized that the creation of a cohesive unit is equally important in teaching skills to the soldier. Ideally, both occur simultaneously, and the learned skills are seen as essential for meeting the expectations of fellow soldiers. The danger occurs when cost-effectiveness managers review a training program and eliminate portions that promote cohesion but that don't contribute to learning a skill and are thus seen as areas in which time and money can be saved. It is also essential that units created through this process be maintained as operational units at the platoon and company level and not be broken up to provide for individual replacements.

The maintenance of unit boundaries and, therefore, of cohesion directly depends upon the frequency with which unit members associate with each other, the perception of a common and worthwhile purpose, and the structure of the group to achieve its purpose and to distinguish the unit from other organizations. Small-unit boundaries must be reinforced by physical surroundings, personnel policies, day-to-day routines, traditions, and ceremonies.

Cohesive units will benefit significantly from barracks and mess halls designed to increase the frequency and duration of unit members' association. Other unit housekeeping facilities and activities should also be designed to promote frequent and extended association. Clubs, athletics, and social events should be organized to promote unit participation. To the same end, unit history, ceremonies, distinctive insignia, and other items representative of unit and national history should be taught to new members and should be periodically reinforced for older members.

Pass and leave policies that are not routine and that ensure that absences from the unit are limited to approved purposes help maintain the high frequency of association necessary for cohesion. In particular, passes should be awarded only to soldiers who have demonstrated solidarity with the group by strict adherence to group norms in their day-to-day behavior. When possible, passes should be given to groups of two or three soldiers from the same unit. In this manner, unit norms are maintained when the soldier is away from the unit.

Cohesive units discourage member soldiers from belonging to autonomous groups with possibly deviant norms. Such discouragement is accomplished by structuring army life to be an all-consuming experience, capable of satisfying all of the soldier's needs during the expected duration of his service.

The soldier must view his immediate unit as the source of the good things in his life as well as the originator and enforcer of strict behavioral norms. Control over pay, promotions, awards, and recognition of all types should be located at platoon and company levels. Although centralized control of these functions at higher levels might be more efficient and equitable, it focuses the soldier's attention away from his immediate unit and detracts significantly from the ability of unit leaders to use such rewards in building unit cohesion.

Finally, the number of soldiers in a unit under the direct influence of competent noncommissioned and junior officers and the amount of structure between soldiers and leaders significantly affect cohesion. The general rules are that cohesion is inversely proportioned to the size of the group and that the more the relationships are structured, the greater the cohesion.

For an army, the key question is this: how far down in the ranks does the formal organizational structure reach? An army concerned with building cohesive units will ensure that each soldier is firmly associated with a group that is a formal military unit as well as the primary influence in controlling his day-to-day behavior. This process is most effectively accomplished in three-to-five-man groups in which the leader is appointed by the army and is the actual as well as the formal leader of the group.

Such a group will be the basic building block of an army organization and will serve as a disciplined, fire-and-maneuver, combat, or operational unit as well as a buddy group capable of meeting the basic affection and recognition needs of the soldier. Such an organization extends itself into a group of soldiers and, through leadership, brings congruence between group norms and army objectives.

In sum, unit cohesion will be strengthened significantly if army policies and practices emphasize unit integrity during off-duty and maintenance hours as well as during training and operations. Unit stability must be given priority within units as well as throughout the army replacement system. Preserving unit integrity maintains the primary group with which soldiers identify. Within units, personnel policies must emphasize structuring small groups under the positive control of competent and respected noncommissioned and junior officers. Additionally, actions of individual soldiers must be controlled 24 hours a day in order to increase the frequency of intra-unit association and the ultimate dependence of the soldier upon the unit. An army building cohesive units will

1. structure smallest units not to exceed 10 soldiers with sub-elements numbering 3 to 5 under the positive control of respected and competent leadership;

2. use a unit rotation system rather than individual replacements, emphasizing personnel stability within units;

3. rely on rites-of-passage processes in basic training and initial entry to resocialize soldiers and form initial cohesive units;

4. maintain high frequency of association among unit members by reinforcing unit boundaries through design of barracks, mess halls, and day rooms and provide clubs and athletic facilities designed to promote unit association at off-duty social and athletic events;

5. distinguish boundaries of the unit by creating a "we-they" view through traditions, ceremonies, and distinctive insignia;

6. prohibit soldiers from belonging to autonomous groups with possibly deviant norms;

7. establish pass and leave policies that keep leave short and encourage joint passes with other unit members; and

8. reduce centralized, bureaucratic control over the good things in the soldier's life and give control of these to the immediate leaders of the individual soldier. Pay, promotions, leaves, passes, and awards should be dispersed and in some instances controlled no higher than section or company level.

Motivation and Control

Causes of a soldier's behavior are directly linked to the satisfaction of needs and values, which in turn can often be determined from a soldier's attitude. Controlling behavior through a soldier's needs and values can be effected in several ways. Three approaches are generally recognized—coercive, utilitarian, and normative (i.e., involving personal commitment). Each approaches the individual through needs and values.

Coercive motivation is based on the need of the individual to avoid severe physiological deprivation, hardship, or pain for himself or for someone whom he values. Such an approach is often termed negative motivation, and the individual is alienated from the organization. The limitations of this type of motivation for an army are obvious. Modern warfare has made the control of troops in combat exceedingly difficult. No longer do soldiers enter combat in rigid formations under the watchful eye of noncommissioned officers who are behind them with swords drawn. Modern weapons and tactics have made direct control of troops in combat exceedingly difficult if not impossible. The dispersion, confusion, chance, and danger that characterize modern battlefields have caused a significant historical shift downwards in the locus of control and have increased attempts to rely on other methods of control.

Utilitarian control is essentially based upon a managerial approach to leadership and decisionmaking that relies heavily upon utilitarian motivation in the form of monetary reward or other tangible benefits. This approach assumes that the soldier is an "economic man," who, when paid enough, can be recruited and induced to do the tough jobs such as serve in the combat arms. Utilitarian motivation is the motivation of the marketplace; individual decisions are made primarily for tangible benefit on the basis of a calculative attitude, with the decision to opt out of the army always a real choice if the going gets too tough. In an army where significant incentives are utilitarian, the commitment of a soldier to his unit is not very strong—no job is worth getting killed for.

The only force on the battlefield strong enough to make a soldier advance under fire is his loyalty to a small group and the group's expectation that he will advance. This behavior is the consequence of strong personal or moral commitment. It represents the internalization of strong group values and norms that causes the soldier to conform to unit expectations even when separated from the unit. The soldier with a strong moral commitment to his unit sees himself in battle or even in day-to-day routine as part of a small, intimate group, represented by a few buddies on his right and left or in the same vehicle, with a sergeant or junior officer who is always near. The normative power of the group causes the strong personal commitment on the part of the soldier that he ought to conform to group expectations, that doing so is the responsible thing to do, and that conformity is expected in spite of the fact that he might personally prefer to be doing something else. Such commitment is often referred to as a calling or, at the small-unit level, as "not letting your buddies down." This is the strongest possible type of motivation for soldiers to endure the danger and hardship of war.

An army that relies on a normative control system, one that brings about a strong personal commitment to a unit and its objectives, will prevail over an army that relies more on coercive or utilitarian control, everything else being equal. An army with a normative control system will

1. emphasize the development of unit norms and values in such a way that unit members are bonded together in their commitment to each other, the unit, and its purposes;

2. refrain from using managerial leadership but emphasize personal and continuing face-to-face contact with all soldiers by leaders;

3. refrain from negotiating businesslike contracts between soldier and organization, or between leader and organization, for the purpose of expressing terms of service or expected performance; and

4. refrain from persuading soldiers and junior leaders to accept difficult jobs or duties

through material reward (such as bonuses for enlisting in combat arms or special benefits for taking first sergeant positions).

Surveillance and Conformity

Once achieved, cohesion is not necessarily permanent. Monitoring the conditions that affect the attitudes and behavior of soldiers requires constant attention. A comprehensive observation and reporting system that effectively penetrates the smallest unit contributes significantly to unit cohesion. Such a system must have legitimacy with the soldiers. It must be perceived as having enforcement of accepted group norms as its only purpose and must be manned and operated primarily by the soldiers themselves.

The goal of this system is to detect, not to punish, the deviant soldier in order to focus group pressures in support of the organizational principle of responsibility to unit norms. The soldier is never allowed to be an individual but is constantly reminded of the expectations that his buddies, his unit, and his leaders have about his actions.

The system for surveillance and for achieving conformity should be emphasized when units become debilitated through combat, hardship, and shortages of qualified leaders. The focus of these efforts must be where the soldiers and the organization meet, at the small-unit level. The reporting system then gives leaders at all levels the capability of monitoring individual and group attitudes, behavior, and adherence to unit norms.

Depending upon the gravity of the deviation from unit norms, conformity is reestablished primarily through two techniques—focusing group pressures and isolation. These techniques are not meant to deal with the outlaw or the criminal but to provide the small-unit leader with powerful tools to maintain cohesion. Isolation from, or restricted access to, all social contact is a powerful conditioner of attitudes. Isolated individuals tend to conform quickly to dominant norms as a condition of being accepted by the group. Likewise, a unit that has suffered some measure of disintegration through combat loss or hardship can reestablish cohesion quickly through isolation, which turns the group inward on itself, and through emphasizing the basic cohesion-building procedures described previously.

Most often, isolation techniques will not be necessary if group pressures are properly mobilized and brought to focus. Group pressure is a significant tool available to unit leaders. Either through self-criticism or peer pressure, psychological anxieties can be brought to bear on the soldier concerning his status within the unit. If the soldier is psychologically dependent for security and other needs upon his relationship with the group, tremendous pressures can be brought on the soldier by the leader who is able to mobilize and direct such pressures. The relief from anxiety that comes from the individual's reaffirmation of his intent to conform to group expectations is an extremely strong force for cohesion.

A comprehensive surveillance and reporting system penetrates an army down to the smallest unit, detects the deviant soldier, and serves as the basis for mobilizing group pressures in order to preserve cohesion. A cohesive unit will

1. rely on observation reports on deviant soldiers, reports initiated by peers;
2. view deviance as a violation of group trust concerning common expectations about individual attitudes and behavior;
3. reject the view of the reporting system as "informing" because the uncovered soldier is not punished but is brought back into the group; and
4. accept criticism to mobilize group pressure and isolation as legitimate techniques by leaders for focusing group sanctions against deviant soldiers.

Commonality of Values

Certain characteristics found within the secondary group or nation from which soldiers are drawn also affect the ease with which cohesive units are built. These characteristics are generally associated with a nation's potential for nationalism. However, the degree to which these characteristics are evident within the small units of an army affects cohesion.

Major cultural factors enhancing cohesion are common social experiences based on soldiers' sharing a common religion, race, ethnic group, age, social-economic standing, or sex. These factors indicate the extent to which basic cultural values are shared and therefore the extent to which they contribute to or hinder communication among unit members. Almost all cultures make role distinctions between the sexes. The extent to which a culture socializes its members to accept women in certain roles will affect cohesion in a unit if women are assigned in a manner that disregards these roles. Cohesive units drawn from a heterogeneous society

1. are ethnically similar and share other major cultural characteristics or
2. are integrated and socialized to the degree that minorities
   a. are able to communicate effectively,
   b. share and adhere to dominant secondary and primary group norms,
   c. do not form autonomous minority groups with separate norms incongruent with army norms;
3. are assigned by sex or by sex and function.

CHAPTER IV

Comparing Cohesion in the North Vietnamese, US, Soviet, and Israeli Armies

Physical, Security, and Social Requirements

The North Vietnamese Army

Food, water, ammunition, medicine, and similar logistical requirements presented major problems for the North Vietnamese Army.[1] Terrain, dense jungle, US interdiction, and an underdeveloped logistical support system severely strained North Vietnamese capabilities to provide North Vietnamese Army (NVA) soldiers necessary supplies. The impact on NVA cohesion was sometimes severe as a series of entries from a captured diary make clear:

> *24 August 1965*—I am leaving the camp tonight. My heart is filled with love for my homeland. I pledge to achieve victory before returning to my homeland.

> *4 September 1965*—We hold no hope of life. No words can express the hardships of our lives. I feel pessimistic and down-hearted. Can anyone understand my inner feelings?

> *1 January 1966*—No vegetables and meat can be found here. We have nothing for food except salt, salted shrimp paste,

and dried fish. How unbearable life is.

18 July 1966—The horrible disease deprives me of sleep and appetite. I now envision so many horrid scenes. My heart is filled with bitterness. I wish I could leave the hospital, but the frightful paralysis keeps tormenting me. . . .

28 July 1966—My sickness does not seem to improve. Who can understand me? What would they take me for?

29 July 1966—[last entry] Time keeps going its steady course. Life remains unchanged.[2]

Compared with US soldiers, however, NVA soldiers had relatively low expectations concerning logistical support. Although individual soldiers defected because of inadequate support, strong unit cohesion was maintained, and there were no platoon-level or higher NVA unit defections.[3] A combination of very strong cohesion and of sometimes skimpy but overall adequate logistical support allowed the NVA to endure.

The military unit became the primary social group for the NVA soldier and as such replaced his family, friends, and all other relationships as the chief determinant of his behavior. The NVA soldier was bound by the expectations and needs of his fellow soldiers. In return, the unit provided the primary social affiliation and source of esteem, recognition, and comradely affection. Interviews with captured prisoners and captured documents show that, within the NVA, the three-man military cell became the group that controlled most NVA soldiers:

> The three-man cell is characterized by mutual aid between members which is based on . . . mutual affection among comrades . . . they take care of one another's moral and physical lives. . . .
>
> The three-man cell is suitable . . . for approaching members and finding out their thoughts through exchange of personal feelings . . . and for applying all the tactics of our army. Every combat and tactical initiative can be cleverly and skillfully applied through the three-man cell.[4]

NVA prisoners, like the private quoted below, also testified to the central significance of the three-man military cell:

> *Question:*   Do you think the three-man cell system helps the men's fighting spirit?
>
> *Answer:*   . . . in combat the cell-leader directly commanded the two other members of

> the cell. . . . By telling the two other men
> to carry out the attack, one on his right
> and the other on his left, the cell-leader
> was able to coordinate their actions and
> keep an eye on his cell.

Within the NVA, the individual soldier believed that he had influence over those events that he and his unit were most concerned with. Because his immediate leaders intervened where necessary to protect him from distant and impersonal contacts with higher headquarters and because they solicited his opinions and judgment, the NVA soldier usually became personally committed to unit objectives. Interviews with captured NVA troops make evident the joint nature of mission planning:

> *Question:*   Were the fighters given a chance to discuss and criticize a plan of operation before the operation?
>
> *Answer:*   Yes, they were given the chance to discuss and criticize. The idea was to get unity of command and action during the operation. Before any operation, a few among us would be sent out to make a study and survey of the battlefield, and then a plan of operation would be drawn up and presented to all the men in the unit. Each would then be given a chance to contribute ideas and suggestions. Each squad, each man, would be told what action to take if the enemy was to take such-and-such a position . . . but it was also the fighters' duty to contribute to the plan by advancing suggestions or criticizing what had been put forward. Thus, the final decision concerning an operation or attack was very often the result of a collective discussion in which each member had contributed his opinion or suggestion.[5]

What becomes clear from such interviews is that the NVA leader—who protected and provided for his men and listened to their concerns and ideas—significantly contributed to their combined sense of belonging to a unit capable of dealing with a surrounding hostile environment. The high priority given within the NVA to satisfying the soldier's physical, security, and social needs

resulted in the NVA soldier's identifying strongly with his immediate leaders and unit. An NVA small-unit leader (or cadre) made
this point clear in a discussion of the sharing that went on between
leader and men:

> As far as relations between the cadres and the fighters were
> concerned, I can also say that close ties existed between them.
> Take, for example, the case of some of the fighters becoming
> ill: often a cadre would take care of the sick fighters. There
> were also cases of cadres sharing their food and clothing ra-
> tions with the fighter. I can tell you that we cadres shared
> everything with our fighters, be it a small item, such as a bite
> of food or a bigger thing, such as money. Very often, with
> our own money, we went to buy odd things that we shared
> with the fighters, and vice versa. If the fighters had the
> money, it was their turn to spend and share it with us. There
> was no case of each one keeping his own possession to himself
> alone, or hiding it away from others. The friendship and
> unity that existed among the cadres and fighters were as close
> as among the cadres themselves.

An NVA soldier also spoke of the closeness between cadre and
men:

> *Question:*   Describe the cadres in your unit. What
>   kind of persons were they?
>
> *Answer:*   We all respected and obeyed our leaders
>   because, as I told you, they were nice
>   people. . . . They always lived with us,
>   ate with us, and they understood us very
>   well. We strictly obeyed any order
>   received from them. . . .
>
> *Question:*   Do you think the cadre knew everything
>   that was going on in the unit?
>
> *Answer:*   He lived with, and ate with us. Some-
>   times, when we talked to each other, he
>   came and talked to us too. I think he
>   knew everything.[6]

The United States Army

Logistical support in providing the US soldier food, water,
ammunition, and medical support has never been a systemic problem to the extent that failure to provide adequate support threat-
ened unit cohesion. The US Army has probably been the best fed

and supplied army in recent history. This record might, however, become a liability. The failure to maintain the level of expected support in a future conflict might cause the soldier to think that the support system was unraveling, and unit cohesion could be adversely affected. The US commander whose troops have been forced to miss even one meal because of the uncertainties of field operations realizes how quickly the perception that there has been a "major failure" can spread through a unit. This is in sharp contrast with other armies, where expectations about resupply are low, resupply is not routine, and cohesion is not affected easily.

The greatest failure in providing for the soldier's needs in US units is the failure to meet the security and social needs necessary for building cohesive units. With the exception perhaps of some ranger and airborne units, the US soldier does not typically affiliate with his unit as the dominant primary group in his life. He generally meets his security and social needs beyond the boundaries of the US Army. The small unit has not replaced other primary influences such as family, friends, and other groups as the primary determinant of his day-to-day behavior. Consequently, the US soldier is usually not bound by the expectations and needs of his fellows as is the case in strongly cohesive units. Other claims from beyond the unit overshadow his obligations to his unit. In such a situation, the esteem, recognition, mutual affection, and sense of personal security required by the soldier are not provided by his unit. In units where these needs are not met, the soldier seeks them elsewhere, often in groups with behavior patterns and purposes that are not congruent with US Army goals. For example, this has resulted in drug and alcohol abuse as well as racial splintering.

The ability of the company, platoon, and squad to provide these basic needs for the soldier has been severely limited by the structure of the All-Volunteer Army. Charles C. Moskos notes:

> A hallmark of the traditional military has been the adjacency of work and living quarters. As late as the mid-1960s, it was practically unheard of for a bachelor enlisted man to live off base. Not only was it against regulations, but few could afford a private rental on junior enlisted pay. By 1981 . . . about one in four single enlisted members in stateside bases had apartments away from the military installation.[7]

In many units, well over half of the single junior enlisted men had off-post quarters where they routinely spent nights and off-duty time. Often these quarters became "crash pads" and centers for activities not permitted on post and hence attracted other soldiers who normally resided in the barracks.[8] Combined with the recent increase in marriages among junior enlisted men, especially E-4s of whom about 45 percent are married, it is apparent that for the majority, soldiering has become an 8-to-5 occupation.[9] Moskos makes the point:

> One of the outcomes of the large salary raises for junior enlisted personnel needed to recruit an all-volunteer military has been the ebbing of barracks life. . . . To the increasing proportion of single enlisted members living off base, one must add the growing number of junior enlisted people, nearly all of whom live on the civilian economy. Like civilian employees, many junior enlisted members are now part of the early morning and late afternoon exodus to and from work.[10]

Because of the limited time soldiers now spend in the unit area, the opportunities for leaders to become a primary influence in the soldier's life has been significantly limited. Because contact between soldiers, sergeants, and junior officers has been significantly curtailed, the soldier's strong identity with his immediate leaders has been attenuated. The sergeant is seen as less a leader and more an occupational supervisor with limited responsibilities and contact with the soldiers under his command.

The Soviet Army

Current logistical support of all types within the Soviet ground forces appears to be more than adequate to meet requirements for unit cohesion. The poor reputation of Soviet Army food has been the target of an extensive program in recent years to upgrade both quality and quantity of food. The Soviet soldier's daily ration is now 4,112 calories, so hunger is not a problem. Goldhower indicates, however, that the quality of food and surroundings still is:

> Despite improvements, many messes are poorly equipped and have old, wood-burning stoves. Hygienic conditions are poor, dishes are often not washed, and the food is *monotonous* and not attractively prepared. . . . The new five year plan . . .

calls for new dining halls, cafes, and tea rooms in military garrisons.[11]

The conditions described above could affect cohesion in some armies, but the historically low expectation of Soviet soldiers and the improving trend in this area do not make the quality of logistical support a serious obstacle to the building of cohesive units in the Soviet Army.

Viktor Suvorov illustrates the Soviet attitude toward logistics:

The Soviet Army has a completely different approach to the problems of supply from that adopted in the West—one which avoids many headaches. Let us start from the fact a Soviet soldier is not issued with a sleeping bag, and does not need one. He can be left unfed for several days. All that he needs is ammunition and this solves many problems.

The problem of supplying Soviet troops in battle is thus confined to the provision of ammunition . . . every regiment has a company which can transport loads of 200 tons, every division a battalion with a capacity of 1,000 tons, every Army a transport regiment, and so forth. All this capacity is used solely to move up ammunition for advancing forces. Each commander allocates a large proportion of this ammunition to the sector which is achieving success—the remainder suffer accordingly.[12]

Basic Soviet assumptions about the nature of a future war in Europe, however, could significantly weaken the cohesiveness of Soviet ground forces for logistical reasons. Soviet expectations that war with NATO would be a short, intense war has caused them to structure their forces with one of the highest "teeth-to-tail" ratios evident in the world.[13] The Soviet Army is organized around a combat-to-support ratio of approximately 71-to-29, compared to an almost reverse ratio for the US Army. Should a protracted war develop, intense pressures on the cohesion of Soviet units would probably develop as logistical support became unavailable.

Within the Soviet Army the primary social group that the soldier affiliates with and that controls his day-to-day behavior is almost always found within the soldier's immediate unit. The reason is that, for his two-year enlistment, the typical Soviet soldier spends almost 24 hours a day, 365 days a year with his fellow soldiers. Leave and other absences away from units are rare and carefully controlled. As a result, strongly cohesive groups or *Kollectives* appear to form within Soviet units. In most cases, the norms of these groups are congruent with Soviet Army objectives. But, in a significant number of cases, groups with sometimes deviant norms appear. The formation of deviant groups appears to follow a pattern within the Soviet Army that reflects the manifestation of broad cultural and ethnic problems readily evident within Soviet society.

The most serious cases of deviance can be attributed to ethnic conflict within specific types of units, conflict due to Soviet Army assignment policies. Units most likely to have problems are those purposely assigned a high number of non-Slavic soldiers. General assignment policies for minorities favor the elite units. The rocket troops (strategic and air defense) and the airborne get very few non-Slavs. In the basic combat arms, the tank and motor rifle units, the tanker units receive priority. Those motor rifle units that don't have "Guards" designations are lowest in priority, get the more "unreliable" non-Slavs, and tend to be stationed in the less important areas of the Soviet Union.[14] Rochells and Patton document these policies:

> Duty in combat units is practically reserved for the "reliable" Slavic nationalities which comprise approximately 80 percent of the Soviet combat forces . . . the few ethnic minorities who serve in combat units are for the most part relegated to support duties. On the other hand, the "unreliable" non-Slavs are the predominant group who serve in the combat support functions. For example, non-Slavs, particularly Central Asians, comprise up to 90 percent of the construction troops . . . they are considered second-class soldiers, receive little or no military training, and are most often armed with only a pick and shovel for their daily labors.[15]

Because the core Russian nationality is only 50 percent of the total Soviet population, the total Slav population together with the Ukrainians and others adds up to only about 60 percent of the total. Because of a growing non-Slav birth rate, the Soviets in 1967 decided to use the military as a cultural melting pot to Russify the non-Slavs.[16] For some purposes, it appears the Soviets have created two different armies. In other words, the Soviets have decided to accept ethnic conflict in certain elements of their Army so

long as they are able to maintain control, further the Russification
of Soviet society, and avoid the dangers of creating "national"
units of all one ethnic type.[17] In the rest of the Army, the more
elite combat units, comprised of more reliable Slavs, the Soviets
appear to have achieved a remarkable degree of military cohesion.
The main point is that for the critical units there is little or no ethnic conflict; their cohesion and control by the Soviet Army appears to be firm. Recent and widely publicized accounts of violent
ethnic conflict, theft of food, ineffectiveness, and chaos border-
ing on disintegration should be assessed with the above in mind.[18]
Two very well-known and respected observers of the Soviet Army
recently noted, in response to similar reports, that widespread evidence of conflict does not appear to be available: "of the hun-
dreds of thousands of soldiers we've seen, none looked like they
were starving or had been beaten."[19]

Drunkenness and boredom do appear to be problems in most
Soviet Army units, but effects on cohesion, if any, are not clear.
There is some evidence to suggest that the socialization process in
Soviet society reduces the effects of boredom and drinking, which
in any event are more tightly controlled within the Army. A former Soviet soldier and knowledgeable analyst of the Soviet Army
states:

> It is commonly perceived in the West that the Soviet
> Army has an alcoholism problem equivalent to drug problems
> in Western armies. This is not true. . . .

> The army has a built-in advantage for its anti-drinking
> program: Soviet draftees are eighteen and nineteen years old,
> thus belonging to a population group with a relatively low
> percentage of heavy drinkers. . . .

> Soviet Army regulations completely forbid any use of al-
> cohol by draftees at any time, anywhere. . . . Penalties abso-
> lutely disproportionate to the deed are meted out if there is
> any proof at all of consumption like the smelling [of] alcohol
> on the breath. They might range from washing the floors to
> ten days of confinement in a guard-house. . . . But no
> punishment, however severe, will ever prevent healthy sol-
> diers from getting an occasional bottle, and their resourceful-
> ness is truly limitless in this undertaking.

> The geographical location of most of the military units
> is always at a considerable distance from towns and stores.

Garrisons have fences around them and check-points whose primary purpose is to see that alcohol is not smuggled in. Cars and soldiers are searched and bottles are broken right away. The distance from the stores and tight control over the soldier's time make the procurement of alcohol more difficult.

Finally, the average soldiers have very little money to spend on alcohol. This is the largest deterrent. A soldier's three roubles eighty copecks monthly salary must cover all his expenses. . . . Although the illicit sale of military property takes place all the time it is neither easy to do nor a mass phenomenon. A soldier with the means to purchase a bottle will always share it with several friends, making it unlikely that any will manage to get drunk.

Although the Soviet Army fails in its endeavors to enforce a strict dry law, there is no doubt that the American Army consumes much more alcohol. The American soldier is allowed to buy and drink enormous amounts of alcohol which his Soviet counterpart has neither the money nor the opportunity to get. If there is a drinking problem among Soviet soldiers, it is that they defy the total ban of alcohol consumption. However, drinking is not a health hazard or a danger to overall military performance of the Soviet Army, nor does it affect a large percentage of draftees.[20]

Pressure in the Soviet Army is intense. The recent decision to assist the Soviet economy by increasing civilian manpower through reducing Army enlistments from three to two years has made time very precious in all units. At any one time, approximately 25 percent of a unit's soldiers are new recruits who must be trained and integrated. In addition, high combat readiness goals are pursued. As a result, long hours and seven-day weeks are the rule with little free time. Boredom and drinking result, but the loyalties of the Russian soldier do not seem to waiver.

It appears that there is less need for the Soviet soldier to be protected from authoritarian "higher-ups" than soldiers from other societies that have a tradition of democratic participation. In commenting on the nature of Soviet society and how it complements life in the Soviet Army, Erickson observes:

A citizen of the USSR today accepts autocratic interest, interference, and direction in all spheres of life. . . . The Russian people have accepted, and still accept, dictatorship without too much complaint because it has been an effective form of government in dealing with those problems which the people themselves have considered important.[21]

Though pressures within the Soviet Army toward disintegration (ethnic conflict, boredom, drinking) have been emphasized in the Western press, they have been, to a significant degree, taken out of the special context of Soviet history and development. Above all, such events cannot be judged primarily by Western standards. Within their own peculiar organization, which accommodates these problems to some degree, strong cohesion does exist among the various nationalities in Soviet units. And some progress toward overall unity is being made. In regard to a particular nationality, one former Soviet soldier stated that he had

> rarely seen such a deep devotion to one another. They try as a national group to be together at all times. They were very good in the military service, absolutely impeccable soldiers, and very disciplined.[22]

Another soldier noted that over time the various ethnic groups became closer:

> After the first term of service, the relationship among nationalities becomes more equal; all become more like brothers. During the first term of service, Uzbeks make friends only with Uzbeks, Russians with Russians, Jews with Jews, and so forth. But in subsequent service, this is levelled out.[23]

The Israeli Army

Because of very short internal lines of communication and supply during the several wars Israel has had with its Arab neighbors, logistical resupply has been greatly simplified for the Israeli Army (IDF).[24] Great willingness on the part of the Israeli soldier to make do with the minimum and give priority to fuel, water, and ammunition while pressing the offense also eased requirements for meeting the physical needs of the Israeli soldier. As a result, cohesion in the Israeli Army has not been significantly weakened by inability to provide high levels of logistical support.

The Israeli Army is made up of three parts: a professional *nucleus* of some officers and noncommissioned officers (NCOs), those serving their two-to-three-year obligation, and the reserves. All elements show an extremely strong attachment to their units, which become, for most, the primary influence in their day-to-day behavior for those on active duty. Even in the reserves, the attraction of the active army remains strong, with reserve members often saying that they are on an 11-month leave from the army. The following quote illustrates the influence the unit retains over its soldiers:

> It is remarkable how many soldiers, boys and girls who have completed their term of service, keep returning to the unit for a chat with the commander, or to see "what's new" with the buddies they left behind.[25]

Other observers report the same. The Israeli soldier's unit becomes his primary social affiliation and promotes a very strong sense of mutual affection and attraction among unit members. The unit also becomes a major source of esteem and recognition for the young Israeli soldier, usually still in his teens. As Samuel Rolbant indicates, the influence of the unit in breaking the strong hold of family and community is great:

> Then at the age of seventeen and a half he leaves home and family to spend two and a half years in the Army. . . . A new process of social integration and development is set in motion, influencing his behavior, attitudes, and tastes. When he comes home on leave his family sadly observe that he has changed. He is intolerant of the old ways, critical of meaningless particularism, and looks upon his immediate environment as a suffocating focus of outmoded tradition. He is soon at loggerheads with his elders and is impatient to get back to camp.[26]

The Israeli soldier also has a very strong sense of participation in the events his unit is engaged in, a sense of being able to influence events that affect him and his unit. Rolbant observes:

> Traditionally the average Israeli soldier likes to know what he is doing, and is an unquenchable arguer. He rarely lets anything pass without commenting on it, invariably getting himself involved in a heated argument with his pals about the rights and wrongs of the situation.[27]

The Israeli Army reacts to the complaints and reports of soldiers at all levels and provides the soldier with a sense of influence over events in his life:

> Every recruit regards it his inalienable right to lodge a complaint which, by Israeli usage, can reach the Chief of Staff. It

is not uncommon for the head of the Army to interrupt discussions at a meeting of the General Staff to inquire what happened to Private Abutbul's complaint, or if anything had been done with it. Heads of corps and front commanders alike seem to be as sensitive to soldiers' grievances as they are about the performance of their formations.[28]

Because the Israeli Army does not have a large standing professional NCO corps, the soldier's immediate superior is likely to be of the same generation, or at most two or three years older. He is chosen because of his superior abilities and aptitudes during basic training. Because the Army has so much legitimacy with Israeli soldiers, they identify strongly with their immediate leaders, who have proven themselves to be the most outstanding soldiers and deserving positions of responsibility and leadership.

TABLE 1

*Unit Ability to Provide for Soldier's Physical,
Security and Social Affiliation Needs*

Element	Army			
	North Vietnamese	United States	Soviet	Israeli
Unit meets basic logistical requirements	+	+ +	+	+ +
Unit is primary social group	+ +	--	+ +	+ +
Unit is major source of esteem and recogition	+ +	-	+ +	+ +
Unit protects soldier from higher headquarters	+ +	+	-	+
Unit provides sense of control over events	+ +	+	-	+ +
Unit causes soldier to identify with leaders and Army goals	+ +	-	-	+ +

Legend: Strong + +
              +
              -
  Weak   --

The Soldier's Perception of Successfully Escaping the Army

The North Vietnamese Army

There was little doubt in the North Vietnamese Army (NVA) soldier's mind that he could not successfully escape from his unit. Even if he could divorce himself from his comrades and the overwhelming compulsion of the group, the constant surveillance by his unit leadership and fellow soldiers made a successful departure unlikely. During normal operations, group cohesion was enough to keep the NVA soldier with his unit. During the few extended periods of unmitigated hardship and dangers, when the effects of cohesion were lessened, the surveillance and constant presence of NVA leaders made departure impossible. Small-unit leaders within the NVA knew their soldiers so well that those who were most susceptible to the pressures of hardship and danger were given extra attention. In discussion, a small-unit leader (cadre) indicated how well leaders knew their men:

> . . . the fighters were watched very closely from the lowest squad level up. Therefore, we had all the information about their behaviour and performance from one day to another. By watching them directly and indirectly, that is to say, by following up the reports made on them, we cadres knew whether a man had really good morale or not. Even if a man pretended or hid something, he would eventually be found out, no matter how well he pretended or how carefully he hid. Take, for example, the case of a fighter having an affair with a female: in such case, he'd of course try to conceal it from other people as much as possible, but finally he'd be found out. The same thing can be said of any weakness—how can it possibly be hidden all the time?

An NVA private who had deserted also testified to the effectiveness of the cadre:

> *Question:* Who was in charge . . . of morale problems in your unit?
>
> *Answer:* My unit had an excellent political cadre. He was very skillful in convincing people, particularly those who worried about their families. He used to get in contact with the soldiers in private to advise and

comfort them. Everyone liked him and
followed his advice. Unfortunately he
was transferred to another place, leaving
the post vacant for two months. If he had
remained longer in my unit, I would have
been unable to leave. . . .

Question: Did the political cadre in your unit do his
                work well?

Answer: They strengthened discipline and pre-
                vented desertion. Only during his absence
                from the unit did many desertions occur,
                mine included. I think if he left the unit
                for five or six months without a good re-
                placement, most of the people would
                desert . . . his behavior, attitudes and
                performance always remained the same.
                He never lost the heart of any soldier.[29]

In addition to the attraction of the group and surveillance by
unit leaders, strong moral and physical barriers clouded any
thoughts of desertion. The unit ties were reinforced by anxieties
caused by ambiguous, dangerous, and often alien conditions
beyond unit boundaries. It was NVA policy to assign main force
soldiers some distance from their home villages and if possible to
separate them from village and boyhood friends, all in order to increase their dependence upon their units.[30]

Transfer and discharges within the NVA were extremely rare.
The unspoken policy was that NVA soldiers were assigned for the
duration of the conflict. Rewards and recognition for successful
service were not expected until the war was over. The NVA soldier
who could not wait and who considered AWOL and desertion had
also to consider the personal punishment he would suffer if he
were caught as well as the significant social and economic sanctions his family and parents would suffer at the hands of the Viet
Cong.

The United States Army

Within the All-Volunteer Army, opportunities to leave
voluntarily or to be "fired" are plentiful; they reinforce the
soldier's perception that he has a job or an occupation, rather
than a responsibility to serve the nation as a soldier.[31] The US

soldier does not perceive significant legal, moral, or physical barriers that separate him from the remainder of society and that
tend to keep him within his unit. Certainly cohesion is not reinforced by an organizational reluctance to grant discharges and
transfers easily, and "bad paper" discharges carry little social
sanction. AWOL and desertion are no longer considered major
breeches of trust with the unit and with society, because of the
ease with which soldiers can now quit.

> Since the end of the draft, however, about one in three service
> members were failing to complete initial enlistments. From
> 1973 through 1981, over 800,000 young people have been
> prematurely discharged from the military . . . the AVF, like
> industrial organizations, is witnessing the common occur-
> rence of its members "quitting" or being "fired." In time, it
> is possible that a general certificate of separation will replace
> the present discharge classification system . . . there would
> no longer be a stigma for unsuccessful service. Such a devel-
> opment would make the military that much more consistent
> with the civilian work model. In all but name, the AVF has al-
> ready gone a long way down the road toward indeterminant
> enlistments.[32]

The termination of the GI Bill and other benefits has also
weakened cohesion by removing highly visible rewards that once
signaled American society's respect for those who served in the
Armed Forces. The more a nation emphasizes and rewards sacrifice and honorable service, the greater the attraction of military
service and the stronger the binding of a soldier to his unit. The
US Army has apparently lost this source of cohesion.

The Soviet Army

The Soviet soldier does not view his chances of successfully
leaving his unit to be significant. A number of factors ensure that
the great majority of Soviet soldiers who enter active duty will
complete their two years of service. There is, for example, widespread support throughout Soviet society for military service. The
Soviet Armed Forces, especially since "The Great Patriotic War"
(World War II), have been credited with saving the "Motherland," and significant public support for a strong defense continues. Soviet Army assignment policies reinforce this attitude by

consciously erecting physical barriers to isolate a soldier from the local population, thus providing him fewer opportunities to leave his unit. A Soviet soldier describes this policy:

> A great deal of translocation is going on all the time. For example, Russians would be sent to serve in Kazakhastan, Kazakhs would go to the Ukraine. Ukrainians could serve in Georgia, Georgians somewhere in the Baltic area, and the Baltic people might end up in Russia. . . . The government is trying all the time to make sure that military personnel will have no ties to the local population.[33]

Once a soldier is assigned to a unit, great efforts are made to indoctrinate him to become a good Communist soldier. Part of this indoctrination involves long hours studying rules and regulations that clearly set forth his responsibilities and that significantly bind the soldier to his unit. Goldhamer makes the point:

> Soviet military authorities believe that a continuous study of the regulations helps to produce conformity to them. . . . Indeed, continuous study of the regulations is recommended by a Soviet Army saying: Old soldier, the service is your board and keep, read the regulations instead of going to sleep.[34]

Upon assignment, the soldier can expect to complete his two years with his unit far away from his home region. Discharges and transfers are rare exceptions. For those soldiers (especially the 18- and 19-year olds) who attempt desertion or AWOL, punishment is swift and severe. A Soviet soldier described the severity of Soviet action:

> Two Central Asian soldiers beat regular soldiers to get their Kalashnikov (AK 47) machine guns, discs, and cartridges, and off they went. . . . Finally, they were caught, and there was an exchange of fire, and they were killed. . . . Special troops were raised to hunt them down; the forests were combed.[35]

Troops who desert appear to be the exception; most did their duty. Reflecting on soldiers of peasant background stationed in East Europe, a Russian soldier notes:

> [They were] very much attached to their villages and families, and would rarely think of running away. Also they are not Western oriented. Indeed, they are afraid of the West because it is something they don't know. For them, Russia and their relatives back in the Motherland are everything.

Cohesion is further promoted by rewarding Soviet soldiers with higher priorities for the good things in Soviet society upon completion of their service and return to civilian life. They are given preference in obtaining housing and jobs. Additionally, for those who qualify for advanced schooling, limits and quotas are not applied against them.

Overall, then, the Soviets have assembled a set of procedures, rules, and circumstances that closely bind the soldier to his unit and help form the necessary conditions for building strong, cohesive units.

The Israeli Army

The Israeli soldier is acutely aware of the moral boundaries that separate him from and prevent him from returning to civilian life until his responsibilities have been completed. The strength of the moral obligation felt by the Israeli soldier strongly outweighs any thoughts of leaving the hardship and danger facing his unit. In interviews, Israeli soldiers spoke of this obligation:

> The vague fear of shame, of possible ostracism or disapproval they might experience on getting home alive unscratched, featured prominently in the boys' answers about their behavior on the battlefield. Everybody knew where you were, in what outfit you served, what you did or failed to do, so that it was imperative to return with a clean bill of moral health, morality in this case being judged by standards of selflessness.[36]

Under the Israeli Defense Service law, exemptions from service and early discharges are the rare exceptions. About 90 percent of the Jewish males who reach service age each year are drafted.[37] Of those who are exempted, the majority are attending long-term, religious training. Others have severe medical, criminal, or suitability problems. Of the 90 percent who are drafted, all but about 6 percent complete their term of service. Of that small number, most come from a semi-annual special draft that accepts young men with lower standards or criminal records. Such recruits are given special training prior to assignment in an attempt to steer them from a life of "vagrancy and crime." [38] For those few Israeli soldiers who do leave their units without authorization, significant legal and social sanctions are applied. These statistics are significant when compared, for example, with similar US figures. First, approximately 50 percent of US males are determined to be "unfit." Of those accepted into the All-Volunteer Army, approximately one-third leave before their term of service is complete without significant penalty.

Special programs designed to reward faithful completion of service are not emphasized by the Israeli Army. The common understanding among all concerned is that such service is the norm. To do less not only violates small-unit expectations but also seriously disregards central Israeli values and obligations of citizenship.

TABLE 2

Soldier's Perceptions of Successfully Escaping the Unit

	Army			
Element	North Vietnamese	United States	Soviet	Israeli
Legal, moral, physical barriers separating him from society	+ +	--	+ +	+ +
Difficulty in obtaining discharge or transfer	+ +	−	+ +	+ +
Significance of "bad paper" discharge	+ +	−	+ +	+ +
Penalties for AWOL/desertion	+ +	−	+ +	+ +
Recognition/rewards for tour completion	+	+	+ +	+

Legend: Strong + +
+
−
Weak --

Maintenance of Unit Integrity and Stability

The North Vietnamese Army

The NVA instituted a set of policies and procedures that ensured that the unit dominated the soldier's life 24 hours a day. The NVA relied upon the three-man military cell to allow the formal organization to reach to every individual soldier and control his behavior during off-duty maintenance hours as well as during operations and training.[39]

Once assigned to a three-man cell within a squad and platoon, the individual soldier could count on remaining with his comrades as part of that small unit. As a matter of policy, the NVA did not use an individual replacement system but recognized that unit rotation was essential for maintaining group cohesion.[40]

A cadre notes the significance of the three-man military cell and of NVA policies designed to keep lower level units together once formed:

> Thanks to the three-man cells, we were able to keep track of the men's morale. . . . It was hard to tell whose morale was the highest when we were at camp, but during combat, whoever was fearless was the one who had good morale. As we fought by the three-man cells, it was easy to check the men's morale. After each battle, the cell leader reported the morale of the men in the cell to the squad leaders who reported to the platoon leaders and so on. As company leader, I got a pretty good picture of the men's fighting spirit.

A private's perception of the usefulness of the three-man cell was somewhat different, but he also recognized its utility:

> In my opinion, that three-man cell system is somewhat useful. When I was lonely in the forest, I could confide to my cell members about my native place, my village. In assignments, men in the same cell could work together, help and follow up one another. In fighting, they fought side by side and covered one another. That system tied three men together, so as to limit free movement and made desertion difficult. The interdependence in a cell was also good for the command of the unit. Since the men in a cell moved together in combat, they might report the efficiencies and deficiencies of their comrades to the squad leader.[41]

Intense, lengthy, and frequent association among unit members characterized day-to-day life in the NVA. Throughout the time soldiers were part of an NVA unit, leaders carried out intense socialization and resocialization programs. The NVA soldier quickly assumed attitudes and behavior congruent with those desired by his leaders and the organization. Through intense group pressures manipulated by unit leaders, the soldier accepted group norms that were firmly grounded in the dominant bonds and expectations formed between him and his fellow soldiers.

In addition to operations, training, and billeting, day-to-day housekeeping chores, ceremonies, and recreational activities were all designed to maintain group cohesion. Passes and leaves were very infrequent and allowed only to those soldiers who had consistently displayed attitudes of solidarity with the group. Association with individuals or autonomous groups beyond the unit was not permitted. In effect, the unit and the three-man military cell became the source of the material good things in the NVA soldier's life as well as the source and enforcer of social rules for the soldier.[42] The importance of NVA policies on unit integrity and stabiliy for the maintenance of cohesion in NVA squads and platoons is clearly reflected in an interview with an NVA soldier:

Question: What do you think of the three-man-cell system? Did that system raise the morale and the fighting spirit of the VC troops?

Answer: . . . during fighting, everybody had the duty to take care of his wounded cell members or move his dead cell member out of the battlefield. During a mission, people in a cell should stay close together and help one another in their joint duty. The three-man-cell system helped the squad leader or platoon leader to have close control of his troops who operated separately. For instance, during a mission in the plain, if a man stole something from the people he would be criticized by his cell members (even) before they brought it up in a squad meeting. The cells usually met every evening to review the daily activities.[43]

The United States Army

The deeper one goes into the structure of the US Army, the greater the personnel turbulence seems to become. At brigade and battalion levels, with the current emphasis on extended command tours, greater stability is evident. At platoon and squad level, however, the personnel situation remains extremely turbulent. At fire-team or crew level—the basic three-to-five-man organizations that should be the bedrock of stability for the soldier and for co-hesion—extreme personnel fluidity persists. A recent assessment noted problems in some divisions:

> There is a 16-percent turnover every three months with a bat-talion turning over completely in 1½ years and this does not include internal reassignments within battalions. The cause is described as excessive overseas personnel demands, but the basic cause is rooted in the philosophy upon which the Army's personnel system is based. Central is the pre-emi-nence of the individual in all personnel programs from re-cruitment through training assignment and quartering. . . . The requirement to maintain forces worldwide caused us to manage soldiers as "spare parts" represented by an MOS [military occupational specialty], with little thought about the impact of frequent moves on unit cohesion.[44]

Recent Army initiatives promise to address the problem, es-pecially with programs designed to bring personnel stability into the ranks, permit unit rotation, and allow cohesion to grow. These programs, however, are not yet fully implemented. Signifi-cant turbulence remains. Proposed unit rotation plans at compa-ny and battalion levels would assist in the creation of cohesive units. Significantly, however, even if turbulence is reduced, such programs will do nothing to address the failure of current policies designed to cause the soldier to associate within his unit and iden-tify with his immediate leaders. The problems of horizontal and vertical bonding or achieving military cohesion will persist as long as these policies exist.

Much of the proposed program is probably focused at too high an organizational level—at the brigade and battalion levels. A regimental system is not a necessary prerequisite for building cohesive units, and extended command tours at battalion and bri-gade levels, although helpful, are not the panacea envisioned. Cohesion occurs primarily at the squad, platoon, and company levels, and examples of cohesion without a regimental system are plentiful. US Army efforts to create cohesive units are focused at the brigade and battalion levels, possibly because most of the ac-tion officers working on the problem are colonels or lieutenant colonels and tend to project organizational solutions at their expe-rience and rank levels.

To some degree, basic training in the US Army has become a rite of passage that succeeds in resocializing trainees and forming strong pro-military norms and cohesive units. Pro-Army attitudes and the cohesion established in basic training tend to be dissipated, however, by assignment of soldiers as individuals by MOS, rather than as part of a unit, as proposed under the cohort program. Cost-effectiveness analysis has also worked against cohesion. Analysts tend to eliminate portions of training programs and practices (such as parades and unit days) that promote cohesion but don't contribute to learning a skill; they are seen as areas in which time and money can be saved.

The maintenance of high frequency of association and structured relationships necessary within units for the promotion of cohesion is very weak in the US Army. A large portion of the fault lies with the personnel turbulence described earlier. Other practices, however, also make a major contribution to this failure. Small-unit boundaries should be reinforced through design of barracks, mess halls, day rooms, service clubs, and athletic facilities; unfortunately, they are not. Instead, cost-effectiveness considerations in building consolidated mess halls and other facilities and Army attempts to attract recruits through motel-like barracks rather than squad and platoon bays are prime examples of policies that have significantly reduced the frequency of association among members of a unit that is necessary for cohesion.

Practices that structure relationships within small units and add to the key nature of junior leaders have been weakened through two developments. First, junior sergeants are often not available and, when assigned, are often not able to gain the necessary control because of inadequate leadership skills and lack of authority (see chapter 8). The problems of one platoon, recently discussed in *Army*, make the point:

> A platoon recently visited had been organized under the cohesive unit program. . . . What immediately became apparent was that the desire and willingness were present in this platoon but the know-how was not. The cadre consisted of an E6 with acting squad leaders and team leaders selected from among the platoon members. They had recently arrived on post and were obviously waiting for the leadership and challenge they had experienced in basic training. They did not yet realize that these were to be provided from within the

platoon. Frustration and disillusionment were only a matter
of time for that platoon.[45]

Unfortunately, this situation is being corrected by promoting sergeants who are not yet fully qualified. As a senior Army official
observed, the result is that "We will have NCOs who are not
nearly as bright as the people they're supposed to be leading"
(*Washington Post*, 15 May 1983, p. A2).

A second practice that weakens the ties between small-unit
leaders and their soldiers is the increasing tendency toward
bureaucratic, centralized control over the "good" things in the
soldier's life. Control of such items as pay, promotions, leave,
passes, and awards, while subject to uniform policies, should be
perceived by the soldier as being under the direct control of his
immediate leaders. The centralization of these procedures and the
diminution of the junior leader's role in their execution detracts
significantly from the ability of unit leaders to use these rewards
in building unit cohesion.

Similarly, unit boundaries are not distinct. Ceremonies and
distinctive unit traditions have been de-emphasized under the
press of training requirements and the general trend toward an
"occupational" view of the soldier's task. Very liberal leave policies and the almost complete abandonment of restrictive pass policies have contributed significantly to the deterioration of unit
boundaries. With the advent of the All-Volunteer Army and the
abolishment of then-existing pass policies, the squad leader and
platoon sergeant lost the ability to control their soldiers 24 hours a
day. In effect, unit leaders have become shift bosses in the soldier's daily existence. Most soldiers are independent of their units
and of their immediate leader's influence for two-thirds of the day
on a routine basis; such independence makes the task of building
cohesive units enormously difficult. The great amount of free
time away from the unit also permits the soldier increased opportunities to associate with autonomous groups with possibly deviant norms. Sergeants, as well as junior enlisted men and some
officers, are using this free time for moon-lighting, a further indication that the unit is just a part-time association with increasingly
indistinct boundaries.

The Soviet Army

Stability and the maintenance of unit integrity in the Soviet Army are based on firm policies that significantly promote cohesion. Once assigned to his unit, the Soviet soldier typically remains in that unit—not only in the same regiment and battalion, but in the same company, platoon, and squad for his two-year enlistment. Leadership at these levels is so stable that the Soviet soldier is familiar with most of his leaders. Should it be necessary, units are rotated among missions, rather than rotate individual soldiers.

From the moment he enters the Soviet Army, the new soldier becomes exposed to an intense socialization process that builds upon many of the pro-military values he has acquired in civilian life. In many respects, this process can be viewed as a rite of passage. The official Soviet view, as Erickson and Feuchtwanger describe it, is that there are distinct phases of the soldier's two-year enlistment:

> the first six-month period, when he is gauche and disoriented, and overawed by the difficulties of military life and the strict discipline; the middle twelve months, when he has learned to live with the system and extracts a great deal of satisfaction from team activities and mastering his military skills; and his final six-month period when his . . . main concern is his rapidly approaching demobilization.[46]

During the passage of this two-year period, certain rituals mark his resocialization into the strong and dominant system of norms governing his unit, his fellow soldiers, and himself. The first of these, as Goldhamer points out, occurs immediately upon arrival:

> When the young inductee arrives at his regiment, a traditional billeting ceremony takes place in the barracks. Sometimes the new soldier is placed next to the cot of a second-year soldier, often one from his own geographical area. He will thus be able to learn from his senior comrade.[47]

An informal passage—in many respects similar to the hazing of new members in other armies and organizations—also takes place at this time for new soldiers who arrive at their new unit in a group. Although such treatment appears to be unpleasant in many respects, it usually succeeds in rapidly building a strong cohesiveness among the newcomers. The nature of this "passage" concerns Soviet authorities when it becomes excessively rough and exploits the new recruit by having him perform duties of older soldiers.[48] Within six months, however, the exploited become the exploiters, forcing a new group through the process.

A very important ritual is held for the new soldier only after he has been in the unit long enough for the political officer to ensure that he understands the significance of the "military oath." The new recruit then very formally takes the oath alone before all members of the unit and the unit flag at an historical site of combat glory if possible:

> As each recruit's name is read out by the commander, the soldier leaves the ranks and reads the text of the oath aloud before his formation, after which he signs a special roster and returns to the ranks. After the oath has been taken, the band plays the national anthem and the unit passes in review. The day on which the oath is taken is a holiday for that unit.[49]

Many units distinguish their uniqueness and create unit identity through a ceremony that has "great emotional influence on the man, and engenders in him . . . the aspiration to endure the difficulties of life steadfastly." [50] Such a tradition in one unit Goldhamer describes movingly:

> The lieutenant who assigns the guards to duty first reads the assignment for a soldier who in fact is dead and who died as a 'hero'; the guard who stands first in line answers 'present' on behalf of the fallen man. In the barracks a bunk is still made up for him, with a photograph of the dead man above it.[51]

The facilities in which the Soviet soldier spends most of his time on and off duty ensure a remarkably high degree of association among members of the same unit. Soviet barracks, mess halls, "tea rooms," and other facilities thus significantly promote cohesion.

Leave and passes are difficult to obtain for the two-year soldier and are often associated with incentives to perform well as a soldier. Significant numbers of soldiers have reported that they were allowed away from their units less than ten times during the entire time they were in the Army. Over half the soldiers in one group interviewed stated that during their service they "rarely" or "almost never got away to 'meet women.' " [52] Often when passes were granted it was in groups of two or more under the control of a sergeant.

During his two-year tour, the Soviet soldier is thus bound to his unit so closely that he has few if any opportunities to join autonomous groups beyond the boundaries of the Soviet Army. This does not mean, however, that the Soviet soldier is beyond the reach of groups within the Army with possibly deviant norms that can work against unit cohesion. This, in fact, does occur in those units that experience significant ethnic conflict, especially when unit leaders consciously pursue discriminatory policies in violation of Soviet Army policy. Wimbush and Alexiev report one soldier's corroboration of such practices:

> Sergeants and NCOs are the toughest with minorities. They can be cruel and even sadistic toward Central Asians. They sincerely believe that Russians are superior to Uzbeks, this creates a lot of tension in the units. They give minorities the bad jobs and the extra guard duty.[53]

Soviet authorities probably believe that these problems of deviancy are manageable and that they do not create a major hindrance to cohesion in Soviet combat units formed primarily of Russians and other Slavs.

The building of cohesive units is also promoted by Soviet Army policies that allow the good things in the soldier's life to be controlled at unit level. Promotions, demotions, leaves, and passes, as well as spot awards, are controlled by the soldier's immediate leaders. Such a practice is especially significant because Soviet soldiers are paid extremely small wages. Two important effects in emphasizing the key nature of unit leaders in the soldier's life result. First, low pay significantly lessens the ability of the soldier to leave the unit and thus remove himself from the influence of his fellow soldiers and leaders (extra money from home is discouraged). Second, through a unique system of spot material awards such as watches and special leaves, leaders are often able to promote desired behavior. Goldhamer describes this system in a discussion of a group of soldiers who had distinguished themselves:

> [They] were awarded individual prizes during a ceremony before their unit. One was awarded a gun, another a camera, a third a nickel samovar and a fourth a harmonica.[54]

Traditional military awards are, of course, also utilized and contribute significantly to the leader's ability to build cohesion.

The Israeli Army

The Israeli Army ensures that the formal organization of the Army reaches every soldier. The existence of pockets or groups of soldiers who are not under the firm control of Israeli Army leadership appears to be extremely rare. To achieve this firm control, the smallest units are structured to ensure the presence of formal leadership and linkage with the higher organization. Much training is done in small groups "not exceeding three men." [55] Once formed, the small group is maintained and functions as a reliable unit pursuing Army objectives. An Israeli soldier from Yif'at describes how the process works:

> They shared the same vehicle all through the war, so they became very close to each other. When ambushed they jumped off the jeep taking up positions behind rocks. Thereupon they were no longer three chatting pals but a commander and two men. "From the moment we were attacked there were only orders and objectives," said he. [56]

After basic training, Israeli soldiers are integrated into units in a manner that ensures that the new recruit has found a "home" in which he can expect to stay for the remainder of his service. The Israeli Army does not regard the Israeli soldier as a "spare part." Once assigned, he is integrated into the unit in a manner that binds him firmly within a cohesive unit and that rotates him in and out of combat as a member of that unit:

> In the Israeli Army it is customary, at the termination of basic training, to mix old and new recruits within the small units . . . the soldier (NCO) with some length of service is able to guide the newcomers in the many arts of soldiering, thereby acquiring respect and authority. He will teach members of the squad what he has learned about the border areas which he now knows well, he will show them how to articulate their grievances, advise them on matters relating to their obligations and so on. He will in full view of his men, be patted on the shoulder by the regimental commander who drops in for inspection. [57]

Life in the small Israeli unit follows a pattern that reaches out and totally claims the new soldier and maintains this cohesiveness for the duration of his service. First, there is a rite of passage, which lasts until the new recruit learns the norms, attitude, and behavior desired by the unit. Training is demanding, and little time is available for other activities. In this manner, the high frequency of association among unit members needed for cohesion is maintained. Maintenance and off-time in the daily schedule are also structured to ensure maximum contact among unit members. The design of barracks, mess halls, and other facilities promote unit association and make it difficult for the individual soldier to withdraw. Various berets and other distinguishing insignia are worn with pride and reinforce unit boundaries. Opportunities for absences away from the unit are restricted and closely controlled. The Israeli soldier can expect to be away from his unit only 4 days in every 90, thus the opportunities to join or belong to autonomous groups capable of challenging the cohesion of the small unit are significantly reduced.

The good things in the Israeli soldier's life are mediated and dispensed through his immediate unit with the commander playing a prominent role, though the pay and other material benefits of the term soldier are small compared to those of the professional career Israeli soldier. Passes, awards, and other good things must be earned and are not easily gained. For example, within the entire Israeli Defense Force—Army, Navy, and Air Force—less than 120 medals for bravery had been awarded through 1979.[58] Letters of recognition presented by unit commanders are much more common and are prized within the small unit.

TABLE 3

Maintenance of Unit Integrity and Stability

	Army			
Element	*North Vietnamese*	*United States*	*Soviet*	*Israeli*
Smallest unit under 5 soldiers and under positive control of leader	+ +	–	+	+ +
Replacement by unit rotation	+ +	– –	+ +	+ +
Strong resocialization process	+ +	–	+ +	+ +

TABLE 3

Maintenance of Unit Integrity and Stability—Continued

	Army			
Element	*North Vietnamese*	*United States*	*Soviet*	*Israeli*
High frequency of association through policies, facility design, and social functions	+ +	–	+	+ +
Unit boundaries established through tradition and long time affiliation	+ +	+	+	+
Control of soldier's affiliation with outside groups	+ +	–	+ +	+
Leave and pass policies controlled and limited	+ +	– –	+ +	+
Control over rewards—pay, passes, promotions, etc. at unit level	+ +	–	+ +	+

Legend: Strong + +
              +
              –
   Weak   – –

Motivation and Control

The North Vietnamese Army

Without a doubt, one of the strongest and most significant factors of the North Vietnamese Army's endurance and eventual dominance in Vietnam was the normative motivational approach taken by the NVA to bind its soldiers to the organization. Rather than the tangible rewards and "economic man" assumptions relied upon for attracting and retaining soldiers in other armies, the NVA relied almost exclusively on an approach that required the internalization of strong group values and norms that bound the NVA soldier to the organization and its objectives. This type of motivation, which achieves congruency between group norms and organizational objectives, provided the NVA with the strongest possible basis for preparing soldiers to endure the hardships of war as part of a strong and cohesive unit. The operative principles of the system are illustrated in an NVA organizational directive:

> a. Organization: . . . We must organize the three-man-cell based on the following principles:

> we should pick three men who are most closely related to one another in their functions and form them into a cell. . . .

> we should insert Party and Group members into every cell to insure its quality. . . .

> b. Scope of activities: include discussions on methods to carry out the combat tasks and missions assigned to each platoon, squad, cell, and members; and examination of the physical and mental life of each individual; and his personal feelings and desires. . . .

> these discussions can be conducted every day, during off-duty hours in the evening, during the 10-minutes breaks of a training session or at the last halt of a movement near the bivouacking area. We can even conduct them while our units are conducting a combat operation or about to withdraw, as the situation permits, in order to strengthen our troops' morale. The themes of discussion must be short, simple, realistic and in keeping with the situation and mission of the cell. . . .

An NVA soldier described the effect of such policies:

> The troops in a unit considered the political officer as their mother. This cadre always . . . saw to it the unit was unified. Besides the ideological training, the political cadres also promoted the fighting spirit of the soldiers and took charge of their subsistence, i.e., food and drink, etc. Because of this devotion the troops in a unit liked and respected the political officer very much. Due to such respect and confidence, the troops could always overcome the difficulties in the fighting, as well as in the daily work, carry out thoroughly the orders of the cadres and achieve good results for the unit . . .[59]

The United States Army

Over the past decade, the US Army has moved significantly toward utilitarian motivation, described by Charles Moskos as the occupational end of his institutional-occupational model.[60] Policy decisions necessary to support the All-Volunteer Army are designed to appeal much more to the personal self-interest of soldiers, rather than to the "higher good" of service to the nation. The movement toward viewing soldiering as just another job, subject to marketplace demands, makes the building of cohesive units extremely difficult. In describing the assumptions that underlie the All-Volunteer Army, Moskos documents this shift in perspective:

> The marketplace premise of the Gates Commission and the architects of the present AVF [All-Volunteer Force] dovetailed with the systems analysts who had become ascendant in the Department of Defense under both Democratic and Republican administrations. Whether under the rubric of econometrics or systems analysis, *the redefinition of military service is based on a core set of assumptions. First*, there is no analytical distinction between military systems and other systems, especially no difference between cost-effectiveness analysis of civilian enterprises and military services. *Second*, military compensation should as much as possible be in cash (rather than in kind or deferred) and be linked as much as possible to skill differences of individual service members (thereby allowing for a more efficient operation of the marketplace). *Third*, social cohesion and goal commitment are essentially unmeasurable (thereby an inappropriate object of analysis). *Fourth*, if end-strength manpower targets are met in the AVF, social organizational factors are incidental concerns [emphasis added].[61]

Current US Army "managers," with some encouraging exceptions, do not recognize that normative motivation is the only force on the battlefield strong enough to cause soldiers to advance reliably against enemy fire. Instead, such managers choose to assume that the soldier is an "economic man" motivated primarily by personal gain. It is not recognized that individual decisions made for tangible gain allow the soldier to "opt out" of an organization if the going gets too tough. In an army where the primary incentives are economic, the soldier is not strongly bound to his unit—no job is worth getting killed for. Elsewhere I have shown that reliance on economic motivation is increasing:

> Marketplace motivation is evident throughout the Army. At the top levels commanders often "negotiate" with subordinate commanders, with results expressed in terms of "contracts." Appeals to join the Army and to reenlist are based on tangible inducements. Re-up bonuses, expensive pay raises and now perhaps targeted pay raises all perpetuate the system.

Even within the NCO corps tangible incentives are now necessary to entice NCOs into combat-arms leadership jobs and to take the job of First Sergeant—once thought to be the pinnacle of an NCO career. It is evident we are turning increasingly to utilitarian motivation which cannot fail to have long-term deleterious effects on cohesion in the Army.[62]

In spite of the Army's plan to rotate units rather than individuals, the devotion to econometric analysis appears to be as firmly rooted as ever throughout the hierarchy in the Department of Defense. Charles Moskos notes:

It would be hard to overstate the econometric prevalence among manpower policymakers in the Department of Defense. . . . It appears that as the technical competence of the Department of Defense to deal with personnel data expands, its ability to comprehend armed forces and society declines. We do not want to be so bedeviled with rival sets of numbers, so overwhelmed with data, that the key theoretical questions are hardly understood, much less addressed. What passes for sophisticated econometric analyses actually cloaks an excessive reliance on simplistic market incentives.[63]

The view of the All-Volunteer Army reflected above is not focused only in academia or among a small number of observers with a peculiar view of recent developments. The view that the volunteer Army has reduced the Army's control and made the building of cohesive units extremely difficult is widespread. In a Congressional Research report, Goldrich observes:

There is little doubt that the extent to which the military as an institution exerts control over its members . . . has diminished substantially over the past two decades. Formerly, this extraordinary control was considered to be a mainstay of military discipline. . . . Certain aspects of the AVF appear to have contributed directly to this erosion of control. The dramatic rise in junior enlisted pay, for instance, has given single enlisted personnel much more discretion. . . . Cars and frequent off-base excursions are two of the most significant examples. The same rise in pay . . . has led to a considerable number of single enlisted personnel living off-base, and therefore, little different from civilian commuters going to and from work each day. The greatly increased proportion of married junior enlisted personnel has similarly diminished the control of the Armed Forces over more of its members. . . . Finally, the steep rise in first-term enlisted attrition

unquestionably results from a tacit policy decision by DOD
that it is more appropriate to discharge a recalcitrant than use
traditional military discipline to motivate him. . . . Put in
another way, the All-Volunteer military, like industrial organizations, is witnessing the common occurrence of its members "quitting or being fired." [64]

Finally, unrecognized by most who serve, the US military justice system has gradually seen a significant change in its basic purposes. Again Goldrich makes the point:

The extent to which military justice and discipline have been
closely aligned with civilian justice, in terms of procedural
safeguards, narrowing of military jurisdiction, and contract
law, began in the 1960s, well before the AVF began in 1973. It
would seem logical to assume, however, that other aspects of
the AVF would reinforce the trend of removing the previous
primary goal of military justice—the maintenance of military
discipline—and replacing it with the general civilian judicial
objective of safeguarding the rights of the accused.[65]

The Soviet Army

A textbook for higher military-political schools of the Soviet
Army and Navy, *Military Psychology*, presents Soviet thought on
how men are best motivated in modern warfare. In a turgid but
definite manner the text's authors forward the Soviet view that the
only force on the battlefield strong enough to cause men to fight
for Soviet goals is a motivation and control system based on internalized values within the group (Kollective).

The psychology of a collective [small unit] is controlled in
day-to-day activity. Its significance rises under difficult and
dangerous conditions. Control of the mental states of primary collectives [primary groups] . . . is a condition for guar-
anteeing the actual conduct of people [soldiers].[66]

Representative of the same doctrine, Marshal of the Soviet
Union Sokolovsky and others note

modern combat has an exceptionally fierce character and will
have a strong effect upon the emotions and feelings of a soldier. In turn, moral-political feeling [group norms] more and
more are becoming the most important motives in the behavior of a soldier in combat.[67]

Nowhere in Soviet writing or doctrine is it suggested that
utilitarian motivation or the motivation of the marketplace is

desirable or adequate for motivating soldiers in combat. The emphasis within Soviet units is for the leadership to work in a personal and direct way with regular soldiers in order to bond them together in a Kollective that will pursue Soviet Army objectives. Official Soviet Army policy underscores the desirability of personal and continuing face-to-face contact between leaders and soldiers:

> Information on the state of collective [unit] opinion as a condition for controlling it: Only great closeness to the people [soldiers] and an excellent knowledge of each man makes it possible to effectively disclose the reasons for a multiplicity of collective opinions. . . . The prevention of individual negative opinions from developing into group ones is particularly important and essential before carrying out responsible tasks and in various difficult situations.[68]

The role of Soviet officers and sergeants is prescribed in order to build the mutual trust necessary among leaders and soldiers. Desired officer traits are officially described in the same publication as characterized by "moral consciousness, sincerity, sensitivity and attentiveness, benevolence, accessibility." Soviet Army NCOs, however, appear to have the major role in maintaining daily, face-to-face contact on behalf of the organization. They are also cautioned not to become too representative of soldiers' opinions at the expense of Soviet Army goals:

> According to the conditions of military service and everyday life, sergeants sleep, eat, and study along with their subordinates. They are also more susceptible to the influence of the soldier's opinion.[69]

It appears that Kollectives develop extremely strong bonds and norms that are generally congruent with Soviet Army goals. Deviancy, however, does occur, and there is evidence Soviet authorities are concerned.[70] Beyond the extensive ethnic problems described earlier, which are a major source of deviancy, the Soviets acknowledge that intense pressures on soldiers accompanied by "boredom" are principal causes for "absences without leave, hooliganism, and drunkenness." The life of the Soviet soldier is not enviable. His strenuous seven-day-a-week routine starts at 6:00 a.m. and ends at 10:00 p.m. He is paid approximately six rubles a month (about $4) and sometimes gets 10 days of leave in 2 years. He is not allowed civilian clothes during his two-year enlistment and must be marched everywhere when in a group of three or more, even during time off. The overall environment of the Soviet soldier is harsh:

> One of the chief characteristics of the Soviet forces is the enormous pressure brought to bear on all ranks, but especially on the new recruits and the young officers. The continuous pressure of a rigorous training process, the severity of discipline, incessant political indoctrination, the pressure for and to acquire higher specialist ratings, the lack of genuine recreational facilities, and the all-persuasive influence of socialist competition [quotas] clearly have a depressing effect on troop morale.[71]

Though the effects of these sources of deviancy that hinder military cohesion and effectiveness are unclear, knowledgeable observers indicate that "when the chips are down" the effects will be significantly lessened.[72] Goldhamer supports such a view:

> A knowledge of the sources of malaise in the Soviet military forces does not permit confident interpretations of the depth or distribution of that malaise. . . . If, as we suppose, despite some loss of efficiency, the Soviet forces in peacetime are not seriously affected by morale problems in the performance of their missions, then we clearly have even less reason to assume that peacetime "gripes" will be of decisive significance in time of war.[73]

As imperfect as Soviet control over the individual Soviet soldier might appear at times, there is little doubt that the unit or Kollective to which most soldiers belong is the primary group in the soldier's life. As such, it is the prime determinant of his daily behavior which, by and large, is congruent with Soviet Army expectations and objectives.

The Israeli Army

The motivation of the Israeli soldier is the strongest possible—his loyalty to his unit and his strong links to his community and nation make him willing to conform to the expectations of his fellow soldiers even when he is alone on the battlefield. His willingness to advance under fire, his conviction that it is the right thing to do, is rooted in the internalization of extremely strong unit norms that make that unit and its expectations about his actions the primary determinant of his behavior. In the Six-Day War, the group held extraordinary influence:

> Soldiers had a habit after an engagement, of shuffling through the dunes toward the road to see who was being evacuated, pressing the drivers of the vehicles to disclose who the casualties were. They seemed to know every casualty by name, and often climbed into the truck to offer solace to their friends. They often had to be driven away to allow the vehicle to proceed to the first-aid center in the rear.[74]

The Israeli Army recognizes that unit cohesion has been a major factor in its victories over the Arab armies:

> The decisive role of social ties and comradeship in the Six-Day War has been sufficiently established by conversations with returning soldiers. On numerous occasions soldiers were asked what sustained them in moments of dire peril, and what had driven them on. Only an insignificant minority gave hatred for the Arab as a motivating factor. Most of the interviewed stressed the need to fulfill their obligation toward their fellow soldiers—"the affiliative motive" as it has been called. In interviews with wounded soldiers in hospitals heard on the Israeli radio, the word *ha-herrah* (my buddies) is mentioned with monotonous frequency.[75]

The Arabs, however, provided an obvious contrast to this tremendously powerful Israeli cohesion. Major General Harkabi, former Chief of Israeli Intelligence and a well-known Arabist scholar, observed:

> The Arab soldier, instead of becoming a part of a team and deriving confidence from it, turns into a lonely and isolated individual. Since social ties are weak, the formal framework holding the unit breaks down under the pressure of battle. Officers conceal food and water, demonstrate little concern for their unit, and show complete disinterest in their men. . . . It is not that the Arab fighting man was not trained or indoctrinated sufficiently; but these precepts were cold and lifeless statutes from which he drew no inspiration. Egyptian company commanders did not know the names of the men in their units, often treating them as rabble, and they in turn showed little love toward their superiors.[76]

The Israeli Army ensures that the strength of the cohesive unit is employed for Army purposes through face-to-face leadership, especially at the small-unit level, where each soldier is personally aware of his leader and the example he is setting. In both the Sinai Campaign and the Six-Day War, almost half of the total number of Israelis killed were officers.[77] The attitude of the

Israeli soldier toward his leader is to "believe in him, rely on him, and expect him to give them the right orders. Therefore his job is not to send the orders but to go with them." [78]

TABLE 4

Unit Motivation and Control

| | Army | | | |
Element	North Vietnamese	United States	Soviet	Israeli
Members bonded to unit through norms and values	+ +	--	+	+ +
Personal approach to small-unit leadership, not managerial	+ +	-	-	+ +
Leader-soldier interaction on basis of trust, not contracts	+ +	-	+	+ +
Normative "service" motivation, not "economic man" utilitarian motivation	+ +	-	+	+ +

Legend: Strong + +
+
-
Weak   --

Surveillance and Conformity

The North Vietnamese Army

For those brief periods when cohesion was weakened by unmitigated hardship and danger accompanied by the absence of strong leadership, the NVA system of surveillance and reporting became extremely important. This system allowed the NVA to maintain unit integrity until normative motivation could be reestablished within the weakened unit. In addition, the NVA system of surveillance and reporting on the attitudes and behavior of each individual soldier allowed NVA leadership to take action as necessary to reinforce cohesion within the unit. Powerful criticism and self-criticism techniques for focusing group pressures and utilizing individual soldier needs for social contact were controlled within the NVA to maintain congruency between group and NVA organizational norms. A significant characteristic of the NVA surveillance and reporting system was that it was perceived as completely legitimate by the great majority of NVA soldiers. NVA soldiers operated the system personally. They initiated reports on deviant soldiers and participated in focusing group pressures against the deviant soldier. The effectiveness of the system for assisting the NVA in maintaining cohesion is evident in the following answers from an NVA soldier:

Question: Do you think that the criticism and self-criticism is good or bad? Do you think it is fair?

Answer: I believe that criticism and self-criticism is very good and fair. It is also very necessary for the strength of the unit; it helps to bring about progress within the unit. Criticism is made in order to improve a person, in order to permit the unit to constantly build itself up in a constructive way. . . . Criticism and self-criticism are complementary: I make a self-criticism, but there are still one or two of my weak points that I refuse to bring out for review, perhaps out of pride. But my comrades will extract them from me, because I can never conceal them completely, however I try. . . .

Question: What did the other men say about the method of criticism and self-criticism? Were there any men in the unit who didn't approve of it or were against it?

Answer: Generally speaking, everyone approved of criticism and self-criticism. This was because we all recognized that if there was no criticism, the problem—whatever it might be—would be left unsolved among the disputants, and as such, it could only cause annoyance and trouble to the unit as a whole. Like a small spot of staining oil, you must wipe and clean it out as soon as you spot it, for if you allow it to spread out, then very soon it will cause great damage. . . . Thus, in many cases, the men in the unit suggested that a criticism session be held if such a session had not yet been called. Apart from the unscheduled criticism sessions, there were regular ones held every month and week: the purpose of those sessions was to permit the men to express their viewpoint because it was believed that everyone's opinion could be useful and beneficial to the unit as a whole. It was expected that each man would stand up and make his own self-criticism. I believe that everyone in the unit was convinced of the good of those sessions. No one ever expressed disapproval on this point. Of course those who had lots of vices and had committed many faults would naturally feel reluctant to stand up and make a self-criticism, but no one ever denied the usefulness of such a method as a means of self-improvement.[79]

The United States Army

Observation, reporting, and focusing of peer pressure on deviant soldiers by fellow soldiers does not routinely occur in the US Army except in some elite units where a high degree of congruency exists between group norms and Army objectives. Deviance or breaking unit rules and regulations is not viewed by most soldiers as a violation of group trust about how American soldiers expect fellow soldiers to behave. Instead, Army rules, regulations, and missions tend to be viewed as part of, and emanating from, management. When left up to the individual soldier, such rules are not included in the day-to-day factors that govern his behavior. Instead, the soldier tends to view his relationship with the Army as part of the traditional employee-employer relationship, with the soldier having little if any personal responsibility for self-enforcement of organizational rules. The soldier who does act to enforce Army norms is seen as an "informer" who "snitches" on fellow soldiers and is quickly put out of the group or worse.

Rather than forming small units with high degrees of cohesion centered around personal commitments to Army norms and objectives, US soldiers appear increasingly to have a civilianized and limited attitude about the extent to which they are part of the Army and are personally committed to Army objectives. A Congressional Research Service report notes:

> The average first-term enlistee in the All-Volunteer Force is not yet socialized into the military environment. He therefore will tend to evaluate job choices according to civilian criteria. . . . These include job satisfaction—in terms of the individual tasks to be performed and the working environment—and compensation and benefits. . . . If the exigencies of military service demand that any of these conditions be changed, then the recruit feels shortchanged or cheated. This may be contrasted with the draft era, during which a recruit expected few if any individual preferences to be granted. . . . A by-product of [this development] is the growing applicability of contract law to enlistment contracts and compensation, training and service guarantees.[80]

The Soviet Army

The Soviets have instituted a comprehensive and sophisticated surveillance and reporting system for ensuring conformity within military Kollectives. Shelyag, Glotochkin, and Platonov make clear the significance that the Soviets believe surveillance and reporting, including criticism, can have in forming and maintaining day-to-day behavior rules for the Kollective as well as in correcting poor ideological attitudes:

> Collective opinion has a particular influence on the soldier's personality . . . deeds and conduct. In directing and correcting the deeds and conduct of people in accord with requirements of the surrounding social milieu, it maximally contributes to forming in them qualities necessary for service and combat. Collective opinion, thus, operates as a regulator of the deeds and conduct of men.[81]

Ideally in the Soviet system, collective norms are to be enforced by all members of the unit. Regulations require all enlisted soldiers as well as officers and NCOs to "restrain others from misdeeds" and to report them if observed. Results are mixed, however, with the greatest burden for operating the system falling on the officers and NCOs with help from informers employed by the KGB and other police activities.[82]

Criticism and self-criticism are effectively employed to focus opinion against rulebreakers. When the rulebreaker is a sergeant, an officer, or a Party member, lower-ranking soldiers sometimes are prompted to report their observations, a form of criticism that does support the system.[83] While the lower-ranking soldiers do not enthusiastically support the system, its overall effectiveness is such that the Soviet chain of command appears to be reasonably well informed of events within units and able to focus enough collective attention to ensure conformity. In addition, as Goldhamer observes, isolation of soldiers from most outside contacts, even when on pass, significantly aids control:

> Surveillance is an essential component of the Soviet control system. . . . When soldiers go on an excursion or to the theater and number more than three, they must move to their destination in formation under the command of the senior man in the group. Similarly Soviet officers are encouraged to take their vacations in groups.[84]

The Israeli Army

There appears to be a comprehensive observation and reporting system within the Israeli Army. It views deviance as a violation of group trust concerning peer expectations about individual attitudes and behavior. The system is operated by Israeli soldiers on an entirely informal basis with no formal reporting or follow-up criticism or self-criticism sessions designed to focus group pressure on deviant soldiers. No guidance is issued nor does the formal organization appear to promote observation or reporting in any manner. But 95 percent of the soldiers queried in one survey concerning their identification with Army values stated that "they felt keenly the misbehavior of other soldiers." [85] Regarding the informal nature of the observation and reporting:

> No less significant in discussion with returned soldiers was the social stigma factor. Men said what worried them most during combat was what others would think of them, or what their friends and families would feel about them when they came home.[86]

Of course, the ultimate benefit to an army occurs when soldiers behave and act in accordance with group expectations, even when they are not being observed by their fellow soldiers. An explanation of his actions in the 1967 war by an Israeli tank commander demonstrates the power of the group even when it is not present. The tanker "explained that instead of trying to locate his lost platoon . . . he chose to charge at a dozen Egyptian tanks, this being a more practical undertaking." [87]

When similar attitudes are evident throughout an army, effective combat behavior, evidenced by Israeli Army action in the 1967 war, becomes characteristic:

> Once action begins nothing is allowed to stop the advance. The troops force their vehicles onward, patching them up as best they can. . . . Supplies other than fuel and water are rarely waited for. . . . In most cases they achieve superiority by sheer stamina, by superior physical exertion and by an almost unlimited ability to rough it for days on end. . . . some went without sleep for three days and nights, and after both they and the enemy were all but exhausted they mounted a new offensive. . . . They overpowered their enemies by their ability to take greater punishment, suffer greater hardships and strain out the last ounce of physical exertion.[88]

TABLE 5

Surveillance and Conformity

	Army			
Element	*North Vietnamese*	*United States*	*Soviet*	*Israeli*
Reports on soldier deviancy initiated by peers	+ +	--	-	+
Deviance viewed as violation of group trust/expectations	+ +	--	-	+ +
Reporting not viewed as "informing," deviant soldier returns to group	+ +	--	+	+
Leaders successfully focus group pressures against deviant soldier	+ +	-	+	+

Legend: Strong + +
            +
            -
  Weak   --

Commonality of Values

The cultural values underlying cohesion are discussed more completely in chapters 5 and 6. This chapter identifies the degree to which these values were evident within the units of the four armies being examined and the degree to which they affected cohesion.

The North Vietnamese Army

Units within the NVA were very homogeneous ethnically. Separate NVA units were formed for Montagnard and other ethnic groups.[89] As a result, the commonality of values and the ease of communications necessary for building cohesive units were promoted. Additionally, although the NVA had women soldiers, they were segregated by sex and function and generally performed support missions.

The United States Army

Significant ethnic and minority diversity exists within the US Army, sometimes making difficult the communication based on shared values that is necessary for cohesion.

Since 1949 the percentage of black soldiers in the Army has increased from 5.9 percent to over 30 percent.[90] In some units, primarily the combat arms, the percentage is significantly higher. The number of Hispanic and other minorities is also increasing. At the same time, the background of white recruits is not representative of American society; except for the last year or so whites have been coming from the least educated portions of US society. None of these major groups can be said to be representative of middle American social norms or of any other set of common norms, based on shared cultural values, that could be used as a basis for promoting cohesion. Moskos sees the problem:

> The Army has been attracting not only a disproportionate number of minorities, but also an unrepresentative segment of white youth, who are more uncharacteristic of the broader social mix than are minority soldiers.[91]

It appears that the resocialization of minorities upon initial entry into the Army is not sufficient to prevent the reemergence of voluntary resegregation among soldiers when they are on their own time. Race has been determined to be a major factor or a "true determinant of social affiliation" among the soldiers of the volunteer Army.[92] Because of the plentiful free time, high pay, and lessened control described earlier, race and other diverse cultural characteristics have become the bases for the formation of independent groups beyond the boundaries and control of the US Army. To the degree that deviant norms (coming from such sources as the use of drugs or racism) exist within these groups, the greater the difficulty small-unit leaders will have in building cohesive units.

While women are no longer segregated by sex in the US Army, there is growing evidence of the advantage of limiting their further assignment to traditional tasks.[93] To the extent that women and men are assigned by traditional functions, cohesion will be promoted. Combat effectiveness and its enhancement through the promotion of policies that further cohesion must be the overriding consideration.

Organized women's groups and elected politicians must be educated as to what goes on in combat areas; they must be made to realize that women in such environments generally cannot contribute as much to winning the battle as can male soldiers. Women in such situations seriously impede the development of unit cohesion. This, combined with generally lesser physical capabilities and field endurance and, in many cases, with socialized role inhibitions that significantly hinder their duty performance in the hardship and danger of combat areas, causes women to become less capable than men in combat roles. For these reasons, the Israelis, the North Vietnamese, and the Soviets sharply limit the types of duty women perform in their armed forces. American decisionmakers must resist internal domestic pressures that have nothing to do with preparing for combat to expand the role of women into jobs in combat areas that men can better perform.[94] Such resistance becomes especially critical during an election year, when domestic political factors tend to outweigh other valid considerations.

The Soviet Army

As discussed previously, the Soviet Army is experiencing significant ethnic conflict. As far as is evident, Army units are not ethnically pure and are not formed on a national basis. This is the result of a conscious policy decision by the Soviets to use the Army as an "instrument of national integration." [95] Significant successes have been achieved, however, in spreading the knowledge of Russian among the non-Russian minorities in the Soviet Union.[96] The cost of such integration has been significant ethnic conflict, especially in those units that are comprised of the most diverse ethnic elements. Soviet policy, however, appears to be successful in limiting the effects of ethnic conflict on combat effectiveness. This is done by simply not assigning non-Slavs to elite combat units and by assigning only very small contingents to support labor positions in other combat units. As a result, much of the evident conflict and accompanying "hooliganism" recently highlighted in the Western press appears to be in construction units and in other low-priority units that have been assigned the great burden of acting as "instruments of national integration."

Hence, ethnic conflict does not appear to significantly impair combat effectiveness where it counts—in the Soviet combat arms. In these units, evidence suggests that soldiers and leaders are able to communicate effectively, to share, and largely to adhere to key Kollective norms; they generally do not form autonomous minority groups with norms incongruent with Soviet Army objectives. The reverse of the above is generally true, however, of many Soviet units of lower priority.

In sharp contrast to World War II, when 800,000 Soviet women played a major role in the Soviet armed forces, today the role of women is sharply limited. By estimate, only 10,000 women serve on active duty, generally in traditional roles such as communications, medicine, and teaching. Because they are assigned to support functions, it would appear that they have little impact on cohesion in combat units.[97] If Soviet manpower pools fall sharply as is expected in the 1980s, however, one solution would be to call more women to serve.[98]

The Israeli Army

The ethnic composition of the Israeli Army is extremely diverse: many different languages and accents are heard within its ranks. With the exception of the Druze Arabs, Israeli units are completely integrated. (Druze units are ethnically pure at the request of Druze leaders.) Apparently, the Israelis have made a conscious decision to use the Army as an instrument of national integration. Whatever the reasons, their efforts have been remarkably successful. For all of its ethnic diversity and some tension between the European culture of the Ashkenazi Jews and the Moslem culture of the Sephardim Jews, there appears to be an overall attitude that the Army of Israel is "one big family."

After a very short time in the Army, the Israeli soldier is able to communicate effectively in the national language with many ethnic types. Because of the leveling socialization experienced within the Army, the Israeli soldier soon shares and adheres to a dominant set of norms that are not peculiarly ethnic but that represent national values more than anything else. In the words of one observer, the Israeli soldier's "prolonged stay in the Army shapes his future citizenship more than any other factor." [99]

While women in the Israeli Army receive a great amount of publicity, their present duties remain of the traditional type. They teach, perform secretarial and medical duties, operate telephone systems, and serve as mechanics.[100] They live in segregated barracks that are well guarded. Though all women are equally eligible under the law to be drafted, in practice, liberal exemptions are granted so that only about 50 percent serve.[101] Although they are regarded as significant in meeting Israeli manpower requirements, their role in the Israeli Army appears to be one of traditional, functional support and is organized in such a manner that it does not adversely affect unit cohesion within all-male combat units.

TABLE 6

Commonality of Values

| | Army | | | |
Element	North Vietnamese	United States	Soviet	Israeli
Units ethnically similar and share major cultural values	+ +	+	-	+

TABLE 6

Commonality of Values—Continued

	Army			
Element	North Vietnamese	United States	Soviet	Israeli
Integrated units resocialized to allow common values and behavior	+ +	+	–	+ +
Units organized by sex or sex and function	+ +	–	+ +	+ +

Legend: Strong + +
           +
           –
     Weak   – –

The following table summarizes the major comparative categories covered in chapter 4.

TABLE 7

*Summary Comparison of Major Factors
Promoting Small-Unit Cohesion*

	Army			
Element	North Vietnamese	United States	Soviet	Israeli
Physical, social, and security needs	+ +	–	+	+ +
Negative escape routes from army	+ +	– –	+ +	+ +
Unit integrity and stability	+ +	– –	+ +	+ +
Motivation and control	+ +	+	+	+ +
Surveillance and conformity	+ +	– –	+	+ +
Commonality of values	+ +	+	–	+ +

Legend: Strong + +
           +
           –
     Weak   – –

CHAPTER V

Measuring Societal Group Effects on Cohesion

COMMON ATTITUDES, VALUES, AND BELIEFS among members of a unit promote cohesion; in fact, some observers contend that similarity of attitudes contributes to group cohesion more than any other single factor.[1] They also point out that if such similarity does not exist, conflict will often result, especially if the group is held together primarily by outside authority.

Incompatibility of attitudes and values among unit members can be altered through intense resocialization and leadership, but such efforts are usually only partially successful. Cohesion can be achieved far more quickly and to a far greater extent within a unit if a basic similarity has previously existed among soldiers' attitudes, values, and beliefs.[2]

The population that supplies soldiers to an army also provides at the same time their beliefs and values. Soldiers in small units (primary groups) are drawn from an overall population, or secondary group, which can be defined as the pattern of impersonal relationships within a large organized group.[3] A secondary group is too large to function on the intimate face-to-face basis of the cohesive small group, yet it also supports cultural norms and values, which guide the behavior and decisions of its members. Developing over time, these cultural values can be traced to such factors within the larger group as history, language, and religion.

If soldiers in a small unit are from a relatively homogeneous secondary group, unit cohesion is likely to be enhanced. On the other hand, dissimilar characteristics within a unit, such as language, religion, race, history, and the values that accompany these characteristics, tend to hinder cohesion.

Potential for Nationalism Indicates Degree of Cohesion

Significant research has been accomplished on the relationship between the commonality of cultural characteristics, the phenomenon of nationalism, and the ease with which cohesive armies have been created among nations experiencing nationalism.[4] Nationalism may be defined as follows:

> A belief on the part of a large group of people that they constitute a community called a nation, that is entitled to independent statehood and the willingness of that people to grant their nation their primary terminal loyalty.[5]

A study of nationalism will reveal that the role of cultural values and beliefs is central to its explanation, just as they are to explanations of cohesion in small units. The degree to which a strong commonality of such attitudes, values, and beliefs can be demonstrated between large secondary groups and much smaller primary groups will indicate the ease with which small cohesive military units can be created within a society.[6] A nation's potential for nationalism and thereby the existence of the basic values and beliefs necessary for cohesive military units may be determined through an investigation of the cultural characteristics of the nation.

Two primary requisites for nationalism are an adequate population and the amount of territory a state controls or aspires to control. There is no recognized minimum number for either factor. Like Israel, modern nation states can be militarily powerful and yet be relatively small in numbers of citizens and square miles of territory. The ultimate survival of a nation depends on the unique circumstances facing it.

Another significant factor contributing to nationalism is a group's sense of a common and unique history and shared values. Generally, a people's history is a source of common values. It will be a force that draws a people together, especially if it includes a significant period of trial such as fighting and winning a revolutionary war or a war in defense of its boundaries. Even more significant is a people's expectation of a common future. Such a history rapidly becomes part of a people's culture. Legends and historical tales become part of every citizen's socialization. The telling and retelling of these experiences by teachers, grandparents, and friends perpetuates a group's history and also passes on cultural values to new generations.

A common language also promotes nationalism; for example, Hebrew. It eases communication among a people for a wide variety of purposes, while also establishing firm boundaries that often distinguish the group from others.

A sense of belonging to a unique ethnic group or race, often with an accompanying religion, also contributes to nationalism. Consider the Iranian resurgence of national pride and unity with its emphasis on the Persian heritage and Islamic religion.

Leadership, too, is an extremely important nationalistic factor. It is essential that the nation is the primary loyalty among the elite of a people. An elite or leadership with loyalties divided between transnational parties, specific geographical regions, or particular ethnic groups or tribes within the larger secondary group is a significant hindrance to the emergence of nationalism and ultimately to cohesion in that nation's army.

The final indication of a group's potential for nationalism is affected by all of the preceding indicators. It is the degree to which the overall population is aware that they are part of a nation and the priority they give that nation.

Just a bare outline of the principal factors affecting a nation's potential for nationalism has been presented here. The detailed work of Emerson, Kohn, and Cottam makes clear the degree to which nationalism is rooted in the basic cultural characteristics of a nation and supports the thesis that common cultural values significantly promote cohesion among members of a small unit.

Effects of Other Societal Factors

The individual soldier's commitment to his political system and to its ideology (such as democracy or communism) and related symbols contributes to cohesion in small units. The issue of why soldiers fight cannot be reduced to one particular reason—neither to small-group explanations nor to broader, fighting-for-a-cause explanations that are based in cultural or ideological causal roots. As Morris Janowitz states, "Obviously, we are dealing with an interaction pattern, but the primary group is essential for the realities of battle. If there is no social cohesion at this level, there is no possibility of secondary symbols accomplishing the task." [7]

Most analysts agree, however, that compared to the influence of the small group, broad political and cultural values are not nearly as significant in explaining why soldiers fight. Leadership, especially great confidence in the commander at the company level, far outweighs any feelings that question the legitimacy of the war in affecting troop performance in combat.[8] Nevertheless, cultural factors are useful in explaining soldiers' motivation and, indirectly, for building cohesion in small groups. Charles Moskos suggests, through this concept of "latent ideology," that broad cultural and ideological values can influence a soldier's behavior. These widely shared sentiments do have concrete consequences for combat motivation. The belief system of soldiers "must therefore be taken into account in explaining combat performance." [9]

Commitment to a sociopolitical system is usually characterized by broad and general statements by a soldier that his governmental system is best. In support of his belief, the soldier points to evidence supporting the inherent superiority of his political system. Examples are the obvious and plentiful material goods of Western capitalism or the classless societies of communism. Such attitudes can further explain a soldier's behavior if they reflect a perceived need to protect the system through actions against another system or ideology (such as anti-communism or anti-imperialism). Secondary group values have their greatest impact on a soldier's motivation when they are internalized by the soldier through the small group that incorporates these broad norms within its day-to-day operating norms. In this instance, the cultural value loses much of its "empty-slogan" character for the soldier and is linked directly to specific group rules and expectations about his behavior and actions.

The soldier's perception that society sincerely values his contribution and sacrifices for the nation can also motivate him and contribute to unit cohesion. Societies that value soldiers reinforce the romanticism and manly honor often seen in the soldier's life by members of society, especially the youth. This value is perpetuated through tradition and ceremonies honoring the military and, of course, through military victories. Materially, societies that value soldiers provide them priority and special privileges in obtaining the good things a country has, such as special stores and access to scarce goods. Soldiers can be further motivated toward successfully completing their tours of service through programs established by a society that are designed to reward and reintegrate them into society in a manner that recognizes their military service. In addition to symbolic awards, programs for further education and provision of financial aid for such needs as housing have been successfully used in a number of armies.

A people's potential for nationalism is, then, a significant indicator of the degree of cohesion that might be achieved in a nation's armed forces.

A nation's potential for nationalism and ultimately for cohesion in its army is indicated by the degree to which the following are present:

1. a large enough population,
2. sufficient territory,
3. a common and unique history,
4. a common and unique culture,
5. a common language,
6. a common religion,
7. a common race,
8. a nation that is the primary loyalty for the elite,
9. an adequate percentage of the population that

is aware of the nation and give it a primary loyalty.

Additional cultural characteristics that complement nationalism, motivate soldiers, and contribute to unit cohesion are

1. the soldier's belief his nation's political system is best as result of socialization or indoctrination,
2. evidence of the superiority of their system, such as the material well-being of the West or the classless society of communism,
3. a felt need by the soldier to protect the system through actions against another system (such as anti-communism or anti-imperialism),
4. broad cultural values and norms that have been internalized by the soldiers and become operating norms of the small unit,
5. the romanticism and manly honor often seen by youth in the soldier's life through tradition and society,
6. special programs to provide soldiers priority and special privileges for the good things in a society, and
7. programs designed to reward and reintegrate soldiers into society upon the successful completion of their service.

Societal Effects on Cohesion in the North Vietnamese, US, Soviet, and Israeli Armies

Potential for Nationalism in Vietnam

POPULATION: With a population approaching 50 million, the Vietnamese are certainly numerous enough to form and maintain a nation.

Territory: With approximately 127,000 square miles, Vietnam has sufficient territory. Geographical diversity, however, could be a source of vulnerability. Vietnam is 1,400 miles long, 39 miles wide (at the 17th parallel), with two distinct climates and highlands and lowlands. Vietnamese often describe the geography of their nation as a chain dependent upon the narrow links nestled between the mountains and sea that connect the population centers of the north and south.

A Common and Unique History: Dating from 208 B.C., Vietnam has had a history of constant struggle against foreign domination (Chinese and French), internal rebellion, and expansive wars to the south into the lands of the Champa and Khmer.[1] Whether fighting an outside threat or expanding into the territory of others, the Vietnamese have looked to their history as a source of guidance and national unity.

A Common and Unique Culture: The Vietnamese people have a strong sense of cultural heritage. The telling and retelling of tales by poets, grandparents, and parents perpetuates Vietnamese culture. Such oral history passed from generation to generation not only perpetuates but strengthens the sense of a common heritage and values that positively affect cohesion. Vietnamese literature and history reaches even the lowest peasant by word of mouth. Ellen Hammer describes how minstrels carry in song the past of the nation, the value of independence, and the exploits of its favorite heroes.[2]

A Common and Unique Language: In the nineteenth century, a new and even more distinctly Vietnamese writing system (*quoc ngy*), which relied upon a romanized translation of spoken Vietnamese, was adopted throughout the country. It was in the Vietnamese spirit of *doc lap*, or independence (from China), that the new language was introduced into Vietnam by Vietnamese intellectuals and helped to distinguish the Vietnamese from all surrounding peoples.[3]

A Common and Unique Religion: Vietnamese religious culture is diverse. Among the most significant are the four great philosophies and religions imported from abroad—Confucianism, Taoism, Buddhism, and Christianity. While the values imported by these religions are generally compatible with Vietnamese nationalism, they have also been the source of significant interreligious conflict and conflict with communist ideology. Consequently, religion has not strongly enhanced the potential of nationalism in Vietnam.[4]

A Common and Unique Race: The Vietnamese have a strong sense of belonging to a unique race. They trace their origins to 500 B.C., when several clans living in the Yangtze River region of China decided to migrate south to the Red River delta and farther after coming under strong pressure from the Chinese to assimilate.[5] Approximately 15 percent of the present population is not considered to be Vietnamese. They include highland aborigines, overseas Chinese, Chams, and Khmers who occasionally came into conflict with the dominant Vietnamese.[6]

Primary Loyalty of the Elite for the Nation: Within the North Vietnamese leadership, the question of whether the nation or the party came first did not weaken nationalism among NVA soldiers. Although evidence has been cited that supports both views, it appears that Vietnamese soldiers saw their immediate leaders as nationalists rather than as communists. The typical North Vietnamese soldier was not aware of any other midrange or top communist party leader other than Ho Chi Minh. In addition, squad, platoon, and company leaders usually explained the necessity of fighting the South Vietnamese and the Americans in terms of Vietnamese nationalism.[7]

Vietnamese People's Perception of Vietnam as a Unique and Viable Nation: Vietnamese of all generations are aware of the Vietnamese nation and its uniqueness. Possibly the most popular legend in Vietnam, for example, concerns Le Loi, a national hero who led the Vietnamese to freedom from the Chinese. Part of the legend, quoted below, was made popular by the Vietnamese poet Nguyen Trai and is learned by most Vietnamese children:

> Our people long ago established Vietnam as an independent nation with its own civilization. We have our own culture. We have our own mountains and our own rivers, our own customs and traditions, and these are different from those of the foreign country to the North [China].[8]

Potential for Nationalism in the United States

Population and Territory: As one of the largest countries in the world, having a population of well over 200 million, the United States is well suited for nationalism.

A Common and Unique History: US history is a strong source of common values for the American people. The strong socialization process experienced by most Americans at schools, at home, and with associates fosters consensus about unique American values and their sources such as the Revolutionary War, the Constitution, the Bill of Rights, and the lessons of the Civil War. More modern US history has also reinforced these values. American participation in World Wars I and II appears to represent a high point of confidence held by the people in the American Way. The wars in Korea and Vietnam, however, with their accompanying foreign policies, have created considerable doubt among the citizenry and government about the reasons and methods of dealing with foreign nations. Such questioning significantly detracts from American potential for nationalism.

A Common and Unique Culture: Although American culture is pluralistic—primarily a blend of Judeo-Christian English and European cultures—most citizens feel and support values that can be described as uniquely American. High among these values is the sense of worth in being an American and a basic loyalty towards and respect for American institutions, among which are the armed forces and their missions.

A Common and Unique Language: Because English is so widely spoken and understood throughout the United States, ease of communication is facilitated among American soldiers and significantly promotes cohesion. Two recent, societal trends, however, appear to work against ease of communications within the small unit and, to some degree, hinder cohesion. First, significantly lower reading and comprehension skills have forced the Army to rewrite many manuals and other directives to grade-school levels of comprehension. Secondly, some minority soldiers do not possess sufficient English skills to allow them to become fully integrated into primary groups—a problem that hinders cohesion, especially if there is also reluctance to learn and use English.

A Common and Unique Religion: The broad umbrella of Christianity that covers most religions in the United States offers some basis for common religious values, which in turn promote the basic values necessary for cohesion. Diversity in values among Christian beliefs in America and also among other religions and their respective leaders can be significant sources of conflicting values capable of hindering a consensus about national values and related military and foreign policies.

A Common Race: Within the US Army, racial conflict between whites and blacks is currently not significant. Ease of communication and general agreement about basic values appear to provide a working consensus among black and white soldiers that supports national values and promotes cohesion. In some units where the percentage of black soldiers is significantly disproportionate, however, reservations are heard on two counts. First, these units are usually combat units; hence, black casualties would be disproportionately higher in the event of war. In addition, the reliability of these units in the event they were assigned a civil-disturbance mission in a black ghetto raises doubts. Neither situation would promote the basic consensus on values necessary in a small unit in a crisis situation. Second, some evidence suggests that when the proportion of blacks in an organization rises above 10 to 15 percent, racial friction increases significantly.[9] All this suggests that although racial conflict in the US Army is manageable, the possibility of significant conflict is not remote. Resocialization efforts emphasizing national and Army values for all soldiers, black and white, offer the most promise in achieving the basic value consensus necessary for building cohesive units.

Another ethnic situation that might become more significant for the US Army is the growing Hispanic population in the United States and its distinctly pro-community, nonmilitary tradition and Spanish-speaking values. Again, intense resocialization and policies that maintain Army and national values after initial training offer the best methods of achieving values that promote unity and cohesion.

Primary Loyalty of the American Elite for the Nation: The great majority of the American elite would generally state that the United States is a primary loyalty. When this loyalty is translated into specific areas, however, support for a military tradition is at best fragmented, a fragmentation that represents lack of a unifying military ethos within American society.[10] Because American armed forces have not played a central role similar to the armed forces of principal European nations, the American elite does not generally recognize responsibilities for military service and leadership. The numbers of the American elite (such as members of Congress and graduates of top universities) who have no record of military service to the nation and who recognize no responsibility for any are large and growing. This situation is in distinct contrast to major countries in Europe where, perhaps because of traumatic histories, armies played central roles in national salvation and destiny, and national elites recognize a distinct obligation to serve.

The nature of America's fractured consensus about what constitutes a proper civic consciousness is seen in the following

composite view, drawn from several widely respected observers
and commentators:

> A breakdown in the cultural legitimacy of the American sys-
> tem has been an object of scholarly analysis and commentary.
> That a significant section of the American intellectual and
> media establishment oppose the basic outlines of American
> foreign policy is a fact of immense importance. It is not that
> they disagree on technical details, but that they believe the
> United States is on the wrong side of history . . . political
> leaders, corporation executives, law enforcement agencies,
> ranking military officers—have displayed an increasingly
> cynical if not outright negative tone. An insightful content
> analysis of American history textbooks in high schools shows
> an important break in tradition, where formerly a coherent
> picture of American history was presented in terms of a
> unified nation. . . . The social portrait since the 1960s has
> been one that is fragmented and lacking a core theme. Re-
> search findings on elite attitudes also present a picture of a di-
> vided and somewhat confused, national leadership. If in fact
> the national elite has no unified consensus about civic
> consciousness, it may be asking too much to expect it of our
> soldiers.[11]

*American Perception of the United States as a Unique and
Viable Nation:* The great majority of Americans have a strong
and common cultural heritage within which the concept of an
American nation is strong and widespread. Unifying myths and
values are plentiful and widely accepted. Exceptions to this
generalization exist, however, among some minorities. If they are
not successfully socialized and integrated with the mainstream of
American values, which give a high priority to the concept of the
American nation, the potential for nationalism will be lessened,
and greater difficulty will be experienced in building cohesive
military units.

Potential for Nationalism in the Soviet Union

Population and Territory: As the largest country with a
population of approximately 270 million, the Soviet Union pos-
sesses sufficient territory and people to serve as the necessary
foundations for nationalism.

A Common and Unique History: Because a common history
is the source of many unifying values, the impact of the various

histories of the peoples currently comprising the Soviet Union makes for mixed influences upon the potential for nationalism within the Soviet Union today. In 1917 when the Soviet Union came into existence, it assumed responsibility for what in effect was a Tsarist colonial empire consisting of many peoples with unique histories. Forces toward disintegration were significant. It was not until World War II, called "The Great Patriotic War" by the Soviets, that a real basis for a unifying and common history became apparent for the majority of Soviet citizens. Hedrick Smith makes the point:

> What makes World War II so valuable . . . is that it lends it-self to blurring the distinction between the devotion of ethnic Russians to Mother Russia and the attachment of minority nationalities to their own regions. It allows propagandists to meld these peoples together in common loyalty to the broader entity of the Soviet Union . . .[12]

The unifying values experienced in World War II are emphasized strongly and great efforts are made to pass them to future generations. Smith again:

> From an early age the young get indoctrination in paying proper tribute to the sacrifices made during wartime. One scene indelibly imprinted in my memory is that of young children, boys and girls of 11 and 12, standing as honor guards at war memorials . . . four children in the red scarves, white shirts, blue pants and skirts of the Young Pioneers stood vigil, rigid as soldiers, posted at the four corners of the memorial. . . . Down a long pathway marched a new contingent, arms swinging widely. . . . The crunch of gravel stones underfoot marked the cadence of their steps as they went through the ceremony—silent, disciplined, intensely devoted to the sacred duty of standing guard for the Motherland.[13]

Similar experiences are common for children of all ages growing up in the Soviet Union. Such emphasis on their major trial as a nation—World War II—imparts strongly unifying values to Soviet citizens.

A Common and Unique Culture: Within the Soviet Union, the 1979 census determined there were 102 "Soviet nations and nationalities," or separate cultures. All are subject to the draft and military service. Beginning in 1967, the Soviets decided to emphasize "compulsory military service linked to the Russian language as a means to create a cultural melting pot.'' This is a significant and difficult task. Not only do the 102 separate nations represent different cultures, but in many cases they represent a past history of armed conflict against the majority Russians. In 1917, most non-Russians attempted to break away from the Bolsheviks, but the Russians maintained the old Tsarist empire by force. The Bolsheviks, however, were forced to organize a federal state system that recognized some differences among the "nations" that comprise the Soviet Union.[14] Subsequent Soviet attempts to break down cultural barriers among the various "nations" and to promote the Russian language and culture as the desired model have, however, achieved some success. A dissident Ukrainian nationalist notes:

> Millions of young Ukrainian men come home after several years service nationally disoriented and linguistically demoralized and become in their turn a force exerting an influence for Russification on other young people and on the population at large. Not to mention that a considerable number of them do not return to the Ukraine at all. It is not hard to imagine how tremendously damaging all this is for (Ukrainian) national development.[15]

The overall success of Soviet efforts to integrate non-Russian cultures is mixed. Greatest success appears to be with the smaller nationalities and partially with the Slavic groups. But the ethnic nationalism of the major Union Republics of the Soviet Union appears to be withstanding Soviet efforts.[16]

The potential for nationalism among the 14 million Russians and some closely related Slavic cultures appears to be great. Smith comments:

> Russians are perhaps the world's most passionate patriots. Without question, a deep and tenacious love of country is the most unifying force in the Soviet Union, the most vital element in the amalgam of loyalties that cements Soviet society . . .[17]

Patriotism is also reflected strongly in Russian youth. Steeped in "warrior" culture throughout their school years, younger Russians reflect a strong love of country. The answer of one young Russian when asked why there is no resistance by the young to the draft and to other dictates of Soviet society appears to be typical: "Just because we dig Jimi Hendrix [American rock singer] doesn't mean we are any less ready to fight for our country." [18]

A Common and Unique Language: Within the Soviet Union, there are 66 separate languages. Many of these were unwittingly instituted by the Soviets themselves in an earlier attempt to separate Soviet ethnic groups from ethnically similar groups and movements beyond Soviet borders (such as the Pan-Turkish and Arab-Islamic movements). Soviet attempts to make Russian the primary language within the Soviet Union have shown some gains. Largely because of Army efforts, between 1959 and 1979 the number of non-Russians who use Russian as their primary language rose from 13 to 16.3 million and Russian as a second language rose by 46 percent. As a result, 82 percent of the Soviet population is reported to know Russian.[19] Soviet potential for overall nationalism is significantly limited, however, because the great majority of the population still use their native tongue as their primary language. During the past 20 years the percentage who do not use their native tongue has dropped by only 1 percent, from 94 to 93 percent. In view of Soviet claims of the great numbers of non-Russians who are learning Russian, it has been stated that "the acquisition of Russian may make one bilingual but not necessarily bicultural." [20]

A Common Religion: Religion in the Soviet Union, despite official persecution and expropriation of church property, remains a significant influence on Soviet culture. Within Russia, the Orthodox church appears to be healthy. Baptisms are increasing and estimates are that approximately 30 to 50 million Russians are Orthodox Christians, significantly more than are Communist party members.[21] Baptists and Mormons are also active. In Lithuania, the Catholic church remains strong. In Armenia, the Armenian church is a symbol of national identity. Within the small towns and villages of the Soviet Union, religious influences remain strong. Further east, the Moslem influence still supports separate identities among the Soviet peoples. Throughout the Soviet Union, religion cannot be considered a common and unique characteristic. Instead, it is a source of varied values that tend to support separate nationalities and therefore make more pronounced the cleavages among the various people within Soviet society.

Within a large group such as the Russians, however, a common religion can be a strong force in support of nationalism—as Stalin found when he tried various measures to rally the Russians against the invading Nazis. To this end, Stalin and the Orthodox Patriarch made joint radio appeals to patriotism during World War II.[22]

A Common Race: In the Soviet Union, race follows the general pattern described above for culture and languages—that is, races are many, varied, and they are strong sources of differing values and of conflict, especially within those Soviet Army units that have been chosen to be "agents of national integration." It appears that a major racial cleavage has evolved between Slavs and Asians within the Soviet Union and especially within the armed forces. The list of derogatory terms used in the Soviet Army to refer to members of other races is long; the words have extremely disparaging connotations. At the root of this racism are deeply-held Russian biases towards other races. Herbert Meyer documents the problem:

> Russians have always been among the world's most race-conscious peoples, with a strong distaste and even contempt for non-Slavs and especially for non-whites. . . . Russians complain bitterly about the yellowing of their country's population.[23]

Within the Soviet Army, there is widespread discrimination against the *churka* (literally "a wood chip," a term that refers to Asians as stupid, slow, and generally worthless), and against the *chernozhopy* (literally "black asses," a word used to refer to Armenians, Georgians, and Azerbaidzhani as well as Asians). Though many other terms are used to refer pejoratively to race, minority groups also have their favorite terms to describe the Russians.[24] Quoting a former Soviet soldier, Wimbush and Alexiev provide further illustration of the dimensions of racism in the Soviet Army:

> From the beginning we, the white people, considered ourselves somewhat higher and with more privileges than the churkas . . . that is why when it is necessary to do some unpleasant work, say, clean a toilet, a Kazakh would be sent and the Russians would make him do it. . . . It was the same at all levels. At a table in the military dining room, Russians

always take first turn. Kazakhs and Uzbeks always the last.
First we will eat, then they.[25]

Another former Soviet soldier observed that "soldiers and
NCOs would insult Uzbeks and Tadzheks right in their faces by
calling them chernozhopy (black asses) and kosoglazgi (slant
eyes)." [26]

Among the various nationalities that comprise the Soviet
Union, race can be an extremely strong force for nationalism
within the various separate nations, especially among the
Russians and other Slavs. But the great diversity of races within
the Soviet Union today is a major obstacle for a pan-Soviet
nationalism.

Primary Loyalty of the Elite for the Soviet Union: Major
problems exist here also, since the patterns of perceived trust
among Soviet leaders generally follows that of race, language,
and culture. Russians are encouraged to migrate to the minority
republics and assume positions of key leadership in the government and economy. Within the Army, the leadership is over-
whelmingly Slavic. Ukrainians are strongly represented within the
NCO corps, and the officer corps is 95 percent Slavic and 80 percent Russian. Non-Slavs are discouraged from pursuing leadership careers.[27] A further worry from the Russian view is the
declining Slavic birth rate and the increasing non-Slavic birth rate
that promises to make the Slavs a minority in the not-distant future. Overall, it appears that the Soviet elite is divided on critical
issues that affect the potential for Soviet nationalism. Rochells
and Patton accurately describe this leadership division as

> a subtle but steady tug-of-war within the system between the
> dominant Russian leaders who are seeking an internation-
> alized Soviet Union and the determined ethnic minority (lead-
> ers) who are striving for increased autonomy. It appears at
> this point that the forces of national self-assertiveness have
> more momentum than the forces of integration.[28]

*Soviet People's Perception of the Soviet Union as a Unique
and Viable Nation*: In a country where almost one-half the population does not use the official language as its primary language
and where the strongest loyalties are reserved for particular ethnic
cultures, the overall perception of the uniqueness and viability of

the Soviet Union must be considerably less than that desired by the Soviet leadership. There are clearly problems of divided loyalties that must be faced by Soviet leadership. Soviet leaders have not forgotten the large number of defections of minority nationalities to the Germans during World War II, but find the process of shifting primary loyalties of national minorities from their own cultures to the Soviet state exceedingly difficult.

Potential for Nationalism in Israel

Population: Because Israel has a population of only 3.87 million surrounded by a hostile Arab population of about 300 million many observers have expressed concern for Israel's survival as a nation.

Territory: Not including the disputed, occupied territories, Israel consists of only 7,993 square miles. Much of this territory is arid and therefore not useful for agricultural or other purposes. Also important is the fact that key military terrain (such as the Golan Heights or the West Bank) is not now included within Israel's claimed boundaries. Occupation of this key terrain by opposing military forces could be a significant threat to Israel. Additionally, the people and state of Israel probably could not survive without the continuation of significant military and economic support from the United States.

A Common and Unique History: One of the strongest traditions among the Jewish people is their common and unique history. One thousand years of national independence, followed by the 2,000-year Disaspora after the Jews were exiled from Babylon, produced a strong Jewish identity and a latent desire to return to their "promised land." "Next year in Jerusalem" became a rallying cry among Jews wherever they were found throughout the world. For thousands of years, the fragmented Jewish "nation" grouped around their spiritual leaders, the rabbis, and the *Talmud* to preserve their common beliefs. It was not until after the Dreyfus case in France, however, that the modern Zionist movement began and that Jews started returning to the "promised land" with a reawakened spirit of nationalism. When World War II, with its great disruption of peoples worldwide and Nazi persecution of the Jews, provided a major impetus for

Jewish immigration to Palestine, Jews from around the world acted out their centuries-old dream of returning to the "promised land." From wherever the new arrivals came, they already had in mind a belief in their common and unique history. It was a major factor in promoting a strong feeling of nationalism in the newly formed state of Israel.

A Common and Unique Culture: Today, approximately 50 percent of Israeli citizens are native-born, or sabras.[29] Because the remaining 50 percent have come from almost all the separate Jewish groups represented in the Diaspora, the effects on Israeli culture have been significant. Most of the newcomers were Sephardic Jews from the Middle East and North Africa, whose cultures varied from sophisticated and well-educated Egyptian Jews to cave-dwellers from the Atlas Mountains. The largest group not from northern Africa came from Iraq. Others arrived from Turkey, India, Syria, Lebanon, and other scattered locations. Their one common denominator was unfamiliarity with Western institutions, especially with concepts of democratic government.[30]

The Ashkenazi, or western Jews, came mostly from Europe. The largest group emigrated from Poland, but sizeable numbers also arrived from Romania, the USSR, Germany, and Austria; lesser numbers migrated from most other European states.

Though the broad and general myths and beliefs about Judaism form a basis for consensus among all Israelis, the disparate cultural values of the immediate past heritage of the newcomers remain a significant source of conflict. Likewise, the effects on Israel's potential for nationalism are mixed. There is a strong consensus on a common but historical heritage that is worth defending, but the immediate problems of conducting the internal problems of state in a group with such diverse cultural backgrounds cause continuing but controlled conflict.

A Common and Unique Language: Language also has a mixed effect on Israel's potential for nationalism. Spoken by most Israelis, Hebrew is the most widely-used language in Israel. Arabic is also a national language, spoken by many Sephardic Jews. English is taught in the schools and widely understood. Yiddish is frequently used by many Ashkenazic Jews. Many other languages, representing the many countries from which Israeli citizens migrated, are heard. While many different languages are spoken in Israel, communication among most Israelis is possible because of a common ability in Hebrew or another language. The fact that almost all males serve in the Defense Forces significantly promotes Hebrew as a common and unique language—a potent force for nationalism.

A Common and Unique Religion and Race: Judaism is the predominant faith, but there are also sizable Muslim and Christian communities with a smaller number of Druzes. The greatest religious conflict, however, appears to be within the predominant Jewish community between Orthodox and other, more secular Jews. The root of the problem appears to be conflict between the very strict religious laws that emerged during the Diaspora, which allowed the Jews to survive as a unique people, and the distinctly different secular requirements of running a nation-state. When the Army was first formed, many in the Orthodox community demanded that two armies exist, one that would observe the religious laws and another that took a more lax position.[31] Compromise and the threat of Arab invasion have produced an army that has substantial religious law written into its regulations yet not to the degree that essential defense measures are ignored. Again it appears that the Army, through necessity, is an instrument of religious integration, making Judaism an even more powerful influence for Israeli nationalism.

Primary Loyalty of the Elite for the Nation: While the Israeli system of government is a parliamentary democracy with parties in opposition to the government in power, there is a broad and powerful consensus on the rules governing the uses and purposes of power.[32] Foremost is the defense and survival of Israel. All internal cleavages one would expect to find in the extremely heterogeneous Israeli population and political parties are subordinated to this one objective. The overriding priority given by all members of the Israeli elite to the defense of Israel, no matter what their background or the constituency represented, is a major promoter of both Israeli nationalism and cohesion in the Israeli Defense Forces.

Israeli People's Awareness of Israel as a Unique and Viable Nation: The people of few other nations than Israel demonstrate in their day-to-day actions the awareness of their nation and the dangers that it faces. Historically, the perception of an imminent and significant threat has usually caused heightened nationalism. Because of their long struggle and tragic history, the Jewish people are even more sensitive to outside threat. With the formation of the state of Israel, a concrete entity came into being that has served since as the object of overwhelming loyalty.

TABLE 8

Potential for Nationalism

Element	North Vietnam	United States	Soviet Union	Israel
A large enough population	+ +	+ +	+ +	+
Sufficient territory	+ +	+ +	+ +	+
A common and unique history	+ +	+ +	+	+ +
A common culture and language	+ +	+	--	+
A common religion	-	+	-	+ +
A common race	+	-	--	+
Nation is primary loyalty of elite	+	+	+	+ +
Degree of population aware of and loyal to nation	+ +	+ +	+	+ +

Legend: Strong + +
                    +
                    -
       Weak   --

Additional Characteristics that Support Cohesion in Vietnam

Other cultural characteristics than those already noted provided strong links between Vietnamese society and the North Vietnamese Army. While the effects of indoctrination (communism) and socialization (nationalism) are very difficult to measure, it is apparent from examining thousands of interviews of North

Vietnamese soldiers that, although both factors had some influence, Vietnamese nationalism was the more significant factor in the NVA soldier's motivation. North Vietnamese soldiers, whether POW or defector, usually displayed a belief that the system represented by North Vietnam was best. They believed that the people would benefit much more from a system imposed by the North Vietnamese. Almost always they felt a need to protect the system against imperialists, as an interview with an NVA private makes clear:

> The Americans were like the French before. The French came here because, according to them, the Vietnamese people were stupid and needed their help. Actually they came here to rule over the Vietnamese people. Now the Americans aren't much different than the French.[33]

Considerable evidence suggests that the rank-and-file Vietnamese soldier did not have strong political beliefs in spite of significant indoctrination designed to create good communist soldiers. Consider the following questions and answers from an NVA soldier:

Question: Did you have to learn about Marxism-Leninism when you joined the Party?

Answer: I did but very few [concepts] . . . I learned only the rules.

Question: What are the books you were required to read?

Answer: None, but they recommended that you read Marxist books. However, you are free to read or not. . . .

Question: What do you know about Marxism?

Answer: A little bit. Marx taught that he will bring peace and prosperity, a peaceful and equalitarian world. Everyone equal. To each according to his needs from each according to his abilities.

Question: What are the ways to get to that brave new world? Did they teach you that?

Answer: They taught me to believe in Marxism-Leninism. Then there would be a general rise toward communism. First socialism then communism. What people ought to follow is the materialism of the ideology. What a peasant should do, a city-dweller should do, a worker should do.

Question: Do you think it is Vietnamese?

Answer: This is very difficult to say. As for me I think there are many points that (are) not compatible with Vietnamese society.[34]

Instead, a strong case can be made that major secondary attachments, centered around Vietnamese cultural values such as nationalism and peasant socialization (such as group orientation, concept of face, and romance and honor of the soldier's life in Vietnamese culture), contained a high degree of latent patriotism.[35] The NVA used such attachments to create what has been referred to as a strong professional army. Douglas Pike notes:

Americans and others often assumed that the NFL [National Liberation Front] army members were fanatics. Because they performed well in combat, it was argued they were highly motivated, which meant dedication to an ideological cause. Thus the search for the essence of this belief. It proved elusive largely because it did not exist. The best of the military units—the Main Force units—were highly effective because they were professionals . . .what impelled them was not ideology so much as professional competence, much like the U.S. Marines or the French Foreign Legionnaire. . . . Their mystique should be attributed chiefly to a unit esprit de corps that stemmed from the consensus that each man in the unit was a superior and vastly experienced professional.[36]

Even Pike, who probably minimizes the effects of indoctrination more than most observers, suggests that it had some effect, especially on the NVA leadership. A small-unit leader's comment makes the point:

I lived in the resistence for eight years, and eight or nine years in the DRV, in a socialist world. It is not a political book which influenced me and formed my political ideas. I think that they grew in me from day to day. Each day a small quantity of socialist ideas entered me.[37]

The NVA offered no special programs or privileges to reward and motivate its soldiers. Instead, NVA leaders worked almost entirely through the small groups—the three-men military cells— to control individual soldiers through the internalization of strong group norms. In this process, the acceptance by the NVA soldier of broad cultural and ideological norms as guiding precepts controlling behavior in the small unit depended largely upon the effectiveness of a unit's immediate leadership. It seemed that "an intermediate stage of personal identification" with leaders was required for these secondary norms to become operative in the small NVA unit.[38]

Additional Characteristics that Support Cohesion in the United States Army

American societal characteristics beyond those required for nationalism provide additional sources of motivation to the American soldier. These sources of motivation are usually based on a soldier's vague but often firmly held belief that the system that put him in the Army and that he is "defending" is probably the best political and social system possible. Usually, these beliefs are the result of political socialization or civil education.

Because there is no program for indoctrination of political beliefs and values in the US Army, American soldiers have traditionally gained these beliefs and values through exposure to the principal political traditions of American society. This process has been achieved primarily through observation, schooling, and participation; it results in what Charles Moskos calls "latent ideology"—attitudes and sentiments generally supportive of the system that have concrete effects on cohesion and combat motivation.[39]

One suspects that beliefs dependent upon a "latent ideology" were present within the US Army during earlier wars and that they supplemented the leadership and primary group cohesion that motivated American soldiers. Moskos found such a set of beliefs, dependent upon a "latent ideology," in the US Army in Vietnam.[40] In another study, he noted:

> The latent ideology observed among soldiers in Vietnam consisted of anti-ideology (a skepticism of ideological appeals), Americanism (a belief that the United States was the best country in the world, along with an antipathy toward Vietnamese), materialism (a high valuation of the physical standard of living in America), and manly honor.[41]

Since Vietnam and the advent of the All-Volunteer Army, many knowledgeable observers believe that the "latent ideology" that contributed to the motivation of American soldiers in past wars has been weakened.

First, in Moskos' terms the All-Volunteer Army's shift toward an occupational model is also a shift away from a professional army. The occupational model emphasizes the economic variables of the labor market over notions of patriotism and over the obligation of citizens to make sacrifices and serve their country. Compounding this shift away from the citizen soldier is an increasing unrepresentation of overall American society among the soldiers manning the All-Volunteer Army. Although this condition will abate somewhat in times of economic hardship—the trend will be "saw-toothed"—many observers expect the trend toward unrepresentation to continue. With it will come an increasing unrepresentativeness of broad American ideological values among members of the volunteer Army. Survey data also indicate that this trend is accompanied by "a growing sense of disaffection from the military system, and a tendency to view military life in more occupational terms." [42]

The All-Volunteer Army soldier's knowledge of the American political system and affairs of state upon which patriotic values could be based appears to be almost nonexistent except for a basic awareness of the Presidency. Moskos again:

> Cognitive knowledge of the American governmental system, history, and foreign policy is extremely low. Left to themselves, the soldiers will rarely discuss any military or strategic issues, much less political concerns. What little political awareness exists seems to focus on the person and office of the President. [43]

A recent survey of high school and college students in the Los Angeles area revealed an alarming lack of knowledge about this country's recent history and its heritage. [44] A journalism major at the University of Southern California, for example, had no idea when World War II was fought. She thought that it occurred sometime during this century and thought Pearl Harbor involved dropping the atom bomb on Japan. None of the students questioned knew when World War II, World War I, or the Civil War was fought. Toronto was thought to be in Italy and Washington,

DC, in Washington State. Other students were "amazed there was a whole array of countries around Russia which were controlled by Russia ('There are? Why doesn't Reagan make them stop?')." The lack of political freedom in the Warsaw Pact countries was news to one "valley" girl—"What a burnt idea," she said. The survey exposed many such shortcomings—the belief that NATO runs the space shuttle and so on.[45] When compared to the deep knowledge of world and of Soviet history that students in the USSR have and the "patriotic" values that such civic education engenders, one cannot but wonder about the resolve of future American generations to protect and defend US society.

When soldiers are asked directly what they would be willing to fight for overseas, American interests rank extremely low in the priorities:

> First, defense of the American homeland (and rescue of en-dangered American civilians abroad) is nearly universally supported. There is, however, a marked drop in levels of commitment to fighting an overseas war in defense of an ally. Second, all plausible scenarios of overseas war—defense of Germany, Korea, or Israel, intervention in the Middle East to protect oil installations—are grouped in the same category of much lower commitment. American soldiers, that is, display a dichotomous rather than scaled viewpoint on their willing-ness to be sent into combat situations.[46]

Based on similar assessments, many observers are concerned about the decline of "latent ideology," which in past wars sus-tained American soldiers. In brief, they believe that "the All-Volunteer Army is overrecruiting from those youth segments least likely to have developed predispositions toward civic conscious-ness." [47]

Accompanying this unrepresentativeness or relative lack of traditional ideological values is an uncertain stance by the contemporary American elite. Instead, as described earlier in this chapter, the soldier is presented with a conflicting set of leader-ship views about what American basic goals and policies ought to be worldwide.

Finally, the shift towards the All-Volunteer Army was based on the Gates Commission assumption "that military compensa-tion should as much as possible be in cash, rather than in kind or deferred (thereby allowing for a more efficient operation of the marketplace).'' [48] This meant that special programs to provide soldiers with privileges such as shopping and gasoline exchanges, privileges that were truly part of the military community and that offered significant advantages in prices, were gutted and made into businesses that are only marginally competitive with civilian enterprises. Other programs that rewarded faithful service and that promoted cohesion, such as the GI Bill, were also discontinued. According to current assumptions, these were no longer needed motivators because ''if end strength targets are met in the AVF, notions of citizenship obligation and social representativeness are incidental concerns.'' [49]

Additional Characteristics that Support Cohesion in the Soviet Army

In addition to those characteristics that promote nationalism, other cultural characteristics support cohesion in the Soviet Army. Possibly the most significant is the socialization process that promotes the ''militarization'' of Soviet society. This begins in the second grade during which each child is taught nuclear war survival. In grade schools, the ''military supervisor'' has a large impact on school activities.[50] In 1962, the law on military training was strengthened through an organization called the All-Union Voluntary Society for Assistance to the Army, Air Force, and Navy (DOSAAF). Military training was initiated in all secondary schools and vocational institutions. Hedrick Smith—author of *The Russians*—describes DOSAAF:

> It combines the functions of 4-H Clubs, Boy Scouts, the YMCA, Civil Defense, the American Legion and National Guard with branches at farms, factories, institutes and in city neighborhoods all over the Soviet Union. It is a vast operation . . . with membership of 65 million. The organization gives courses in military history and tactics, develops civil defense facilities, teaches youngsters to drive and maintain all kinds of vehicles, to operate and maintain radios and electrical equipment, to make and design aircraft models, to make parachute jumps, to shoot and to learn professions which have military importance.[51]

After graduation at the age of 18, the Soviet male expects to enter the military for two years. If he is college material, he either attends a military school (of which there are about 140) or a civilian institution where his military training continues and he becomes a reserve officer.[52] Each year the active Soviet military discharges almost 2 million men into the reserves where skills are maintained to make available a ready reserve numbering over 25 million.[53] Even though the romanticism and manly honor formerly associated with the soldier's life has probably dissipated, the Soviet male expects to be involved with the military indefinitely. As one observer puts it:

> Throughout his adult life, the omnipresence of the military will strike him as normal, to be expected. He does not see the military as a thing apart but as something of which he is a part.[54]

In spite of racial conflict and other sources of significant dissatisfaction there does not appear to be a discernible desire to change the systems. In fact, many observers state that both Soviet soldiers and citizens believe that their political system is the best for the Soviet people. There is also an often and strongly expressed need to protect and defend the system, both militarily and verbally.

Ideological indoctrination and socialization produce a strong "latent" patriotism; they are credited with the Soviet soldier's pro-system outlook. While the Soviet soldier is exposed to an extremely intense and comprehensive program of indoctrination, the results are difficult to measure. Political apathy appears to be widespread; [55] however, contributions to an underlying "latent" pro-Soviet attitude may be reinforced. This might be especially true when indoctrination stresses themes such as a "love for the motherland," "hate the enemy," and "the cruelty of American imperialism in Vietnam" instead of basic Marxist-Leninist principles.

Other interrelated reasons are probably more responsible for the Soviet soldier's basic satisfaction with the system and his willingness to defend it.[56] First, until very recently, economic conditions and the standard of living in the Soviet Union have increased substantially each nonwar year since the Revolution in 1917. Since World War II, Soviet economic growth has been impressive by any standard. By comparison with previous conditions, the current situation satisfies the Soviet people. Second, since World War II, the Soviet Army has become an immensely respected and popular institution in the Soviet Union. John Erickson notes:

> Wherever one goes in the USSR, one's attention is invariably drawn to massive memorials of the 1941–45 war and the victory over fascist Germany. Everywhere the armed forces are in evidence and everywhere they receive official praise and glory.[57]

The great love of the motherland expressed by the Russian *rodina*, an extremely emotional word for most Russians, also connotes good feelings toward the Army that defends it. According to Hedrick Smith, what makes World War II (and indirectly the Army) so valuable as a propaganda theme is the blurring of patriotism and politics:

> [World War II] enables them to fuzz the line between patriotic pride in the national military victory over the Nazis and political commitment to the Soviet system. In the propaganda of the Great Patriotic War, patriotism and politics are thus fused.[58]

Another cultural characteristic of significant importance in understanding the Soviet soldier's acceptance of the Army and the great legitimacy he gives to it is the desire of the Soviet people for firm control and autocratic leadership. Erickson and Feuchtwanger make the point:

> In the main, the Russian people have accepted, and still accept, dictatorship without too much complaint because it has been an effective form of government in dealing with those problems which the people themselves have considered important. A citizen of the USSR today accepts autocratic interest, interference, and direction in all spheres of life and throughout every stage of his development.[59]

An authoritative mind set is a central part of the Soviet citizen's political culture: as Smith observes, "Brezhnev and the simple person both think that might is right." [60] Nowhere in Soviet culture are there notions that characterize the values of Western democracies. Andrei Amalrik, the dissident Soviet historian, wrote:

> The idea of self-government, of equality before the law and of personal freedom—and the responsibility that goes with these—are almost completely incomprehensible to the Russian people.[61]

Finally, the Soviet cultural characteristic that clearly puts the individual and his needs second to the group or collective is a significant factor that promotes cohesion in the Soviet Army.[62] Soviet military texts extensively describe methods for using the power of the collective to control the attitudes and behavior of Soviet soldiers.[63] Criticism and self-criticism sessions before the Kollective of the small unit are among the most powerful means the Army has for controlling behavior.[64]

Additional Characteristics that Support Cohesion in the Israeli Army

The Israeli soldier has a strong belief that his particular system is best. A 1968 survey among Israeli soldiers disclosed this strong cultural value and related it to the Israeli Army and its purpose. No soldier surveyed thought the Israeli Army was less effective than any other army; "98 percent thought that the Israeli Army was in some or in many ways better than other armies, while 2 percent thought it was better in every respect." [65]

The confidence expressed in the capabilities of the Israeli Army and its purposes is not the result of indoctrination or an extensive educational program directed at the Israeli soldier. Rather, it appears to be the result of a very strong "latent ideology":

> The average conscript is rather contemptuous of patriotic propaganda of the "fight for your homeland" type, and disdainfully calls it "Zionist" stuff. Says a platoon commander in a discussion on motivation: "The moment I talk to the new conscripts about the homeland I strike a landmine. So I keep quiet. Instead I try to make soldiers out of them. I give them hell from morning to sunset. They begin to curse me, curse the army, curse the state. Then they begin to curse together, and become a truly cohesive group, a unit, a fighting unit." [66]

Behind this rejection of political indoctrination, however, is an extremely strong "latent ideology" with 90 percent of the conscripts and reservists questioned stating that they felt a strong need to protect Israel. Most also said they would have joined the Army even if it had not been required.[67]

TABLE 9

Additional Cultural Characteristics that Promote Cohesion

	Army			
Element	*North Vietnamese*	*United States*	*Soviet*	*Israeli*
Soldiers' belief their political system is best through socialization or indoctrination	+ +	+ +	+	+ +
Evidence offered for superiority of system, e.g., material well being	+ +	+ +	+ +	+ +
A felt need to protect the system through anti-actions, e.g., anti-communism, anti-capitalism.	+ +	+ +	+ +	+ +
Broad cultural norms and values internalized and controlling soldier's behavior	+ +	–	+	+ +
Romanticism and manly honor associated with the soldier's life	+	+	+	+ +
Special privileges and programs for soldiers by society	–	+	+ +	+
Special programs to reward and reintegrate soldier after service	–	+	+ +	+

Legend: Strong + +
              +
              –
     Weak   – –

CHAPTER VII

Leadership in Cohesive Units

THE EFFECTIVE CONTROL OF SOLDIERS in combat and in peace is complex and difficult. The nature of modern war has dictated a significant shift over the past 100 years from methods of control dependent upon physical domination of the soldier to those that rely on internalized discipline within the soldier. Today's warfare no longer allows mass formations to attack under the watchful eyes and control of sergeants and officers. Modern leaders no longer bivouac well before darkness or during periods of fog or low visibility in order to prevent mass desertions. The requirements of leadership have changed significantly since the time when the armies of Frederick the Great marched in Europe. The many requirements for small and independent unit actions have deemphasized strict discipline, rote training, and drill. The dispersion, confusion, danger, and hardship that characterize modern battlefields have made it essential to gain control of the individual soldier through the process of internalizing values and codes of behavior that cause the soldier to act as a reliable member of his unit in combat. Because the source of the soldier's values and codes is the small group and because the only force strong enough to make the soldier willing to advance under fire is his loyalty to the small group and that group's expectation that he will advance, it becomes the primary task of the organization to control the small fighting group through its leaders.

Training and situation drills assist the leader in building cohesive units. The confidence that characterizes well-trained troops, especially that training validated in combat, is significant; the soldier needs to feel that he is part of a group that can successfully meet and survive most situations found on the battlefield. The drill aspect of training also contributes by helping the soldier overcome the often immobilizing fear experienced in combat operations (e.g., airborne) and by helping him take appropriate actions expected by the group. Outside threats perceived by the group also cause it to coalesce and pull together to face the common danger. It is leadership, however, that is the most critical factor in building cohesive units.[1]

Characteristics of Leadership in Cohesive Units

Leadership that is most effective in building cohesive units has several characteristics. Of primary importance is that it is not managerial in approach. Instead, it emphasizes personal, empathic, and continuing face-to-face contact with all soldiers in the unit. Because the leader's ability to develop fully professional relationships is limited to a small number of soldiers, units must necessarily be small if leaders are to have maximum impact. An army's maximum leadership efforts must be focused at the small-unit level where the leader makes the link between the formal organization and the fighting soldier—at the squad, platoon, and company level. Above these levels, more emphasis on a managerial approach is required. The transition from leadership to managerial styles is a problem for some armies. The correct style depends primarily on the level of the organization being led or managed. Many armies tend to adopt one approach and apply it inflexibly at all levels. The most evident example is that of the French Army between the World Wars. Personal leadership and example, along with the spirit of the offense, under the slogan of "Elan!" were thought to be appropriate for all levels, especially among the field grade ranks. As a result, strategy and management were not adequately considered, resulting in the major debacle suffered by the French Army at the hands of the German Wehrmacht in World War II.

Few armies today adequately make the required transition from the major emphasis on leadership required at lower-level units to the very different managerial and strategic emphasis required at higher levels of command. For example, the assumption that because an officer was a first-rate company commander he will also be an outstanding battalion, brigade, or division commander is not warranted. Different skills are required. But in building a cohesive army, leadership skills at company and lower-level units are the most critical and must be given priority.

Leaders at the small-unit level in a cohesive unit should have a degree of charisma—not glibness, but the ability to guide the unit gracefully in repeatedly surviving difficult situations. In battle, nothing succeeds like success. Men in danger become acutely aware of the qualities of their leaders. They desire leadership so their immediate needs can be met and their anxieties controlled.[2] In this regard, well-trained and respected company grade officers and sergeants relay a sense of competence and security to their soldiers and, if successful over a period of time, gain a degree of influence and control over members of their units often associated with charismatic leaders.

Casualties can significantly weaken group cohesion, especially casualties that are considered "wasteful" by soldiers in the unit and that are attributed to leadership failure or unreasonable missions.[3] Such a situation puts the unit leader in a difficult position between his requirement to complete his assigned mission and his duty to maintain the integrity and welfare of the unit. In their linking function between soldier and organization, leaders must be perceived by unit members as protecting them from harassment and unrealistic missions from above.

In addition to building upon success, the unit leader must act to neutralize the effects of failure. In success or failure, the leader uses the perception of outside threat or difficult challenges to mobilize and coalesce the unit. The effects of failure can vary considerably, depending upon whether the unit is in the front line or in the rear.[4] When cohesion has been seriously impaired, soldiers will still fight for survival, and this need can be used by the unit leader as a basis for rebuilding cohesion. The soldier's individual need for self-preservation affects his relations within his unit. He recognizes that his chances of survival are greater if he shares the danger within a limited range of tasks that must be accomplished to improve overall unit chances for survival.[5]

The Effect of Ideology

Indoctrination or civic education is most effective in getting the soldier to the battle and in assisting him to withstand further combat after the battle. During the battle, ideology appears to have significantly less influence in controlling a soldier's behavior.[6] Additionally, there is some evidence that soldiers well versed in ideology are better able to resist and to stop the spread of demoralization.[7] Whatever the ultimate effect of ideology or civic education, it is dependent upon unit leaders. Successful and competent leaders who make certain that all unit members share equally in the hardship and danger facing the unit and who set the example will be successful in imparting ideology. In many cases, broad ideological slogans and goals have become specific operational rules of behavior within small units.[8]

An essential requirement is that first-line leaders have authority to implement the policies and procedures necessary for the creation of cohesive units. If authority is centralized at higher levels of command for political or economic reasons, small-unit leaders often are left without the means to execute their responsibility. As a result, soldiers quickly see that the sources of good things in their life are not controlled by their immediate leaders. Promotions, pay, leave, passes, job assignments, billeting, and messing policies are sources of influence for small-unit leaders. When control of these personnel actions is removed from the leader, his ability to create cohesive units becomes significantly impaired.[9]

On Understanding Leadership and Cohesion

Many approaches to and definitions of leadership have been offered. The purpose here is not to offer another but to relate leadership to cohesion in military units by synthesizing available knowledge about the individual soldier, the small group, the organization, and the leadership itself.

Military leadership involves enduring—and primary—personal relationships between a leader and soldiers. Many officers appear to believe that inspiring talks and appearances by brigadiers and colonels offer the best examples of leadership. On the contrary, the vital leadership role is consistent competence at the squad, platoon, and company levels by company grade sergeants and officers. It is at this level where the phenomenon of leadership takes place because it is here that the individual soldier is persuaded to pursue goals that are often in direct conflict with his own best interests. The individual's need for cover from enemy fire, for example, is in direct conflict with the organizational requirement to advance toward an enemy position and defeat it. The primary function of small-unit leadership is to bring about congruence between the requirements of the organization and the needs of the individual soldier. The leader must bring about internalized values and discipline within the soldier to enable him to overcome his fear and expose himself to enemy fire. To accomplish this task, the leader must create and accommodate the soldier's needs by developing a group within his unit whose norms and procedures are strongly congruent with organizational objectives. Ideally, the soldier will pursue Army goals in satisfying his individual needs. The key is similarity of values among soldier, leader, and organization so that such values become the primary guide for the soldier's day-to-day behavior. Therefore, units organized on the basis of similar values have a much better chance at congruence with organizational objectives. If this is not possible, extensive efforts must be made to socialize all soldiers into the desired value system of the group. The greater the effectiveness of these efforts the less formal controls will be required within the unit.[10]

The Leadership Model

The following model describes the leadership function for achieving congruence of primary values among soldiers, leaders, and organization. See figure 1.

Leadership, then, may be defined as the phenomenon that occurs when the influence of A (the leader) causes B (the group) to perform C (goal-directed behavior) when B would not have performed C had it not been for the influence of A.[11]

Interaction between the leader (A) and the group (B) is signified by the two arrows and indicates the exercise of influence

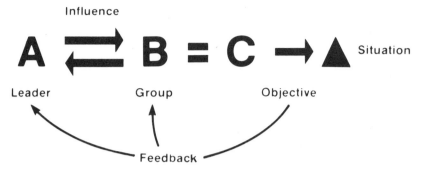

Figure 1. Leadership Model.

through which the leader creates and uses norms for directing behavior within the group. The arrows also indicate the leader's perceptions of group needs upon which the norms are based. The behavior depicted by C is mission-oriented activity desired by the leader, as the agent of the organization, and performed by the group. Feedback enables the leader and the group to adjust their behavior and activities over time as the situation changes.

Sources of Leader Influence

Leaders of cohesive units have several bases of power that are the sources of the influence necessary to control and direct the group.[12] These may be placed into several categories evident at the squad, platoon, and company levels: (1) reward and coercive power, (2) legitimate power, (3) referent power, and (4) expert power.

Reward and Coercive Power

Reward and coercive powers are available to all armies. They may be defined as the ability to exert influence in personal relationships based upon the ability to reward and punish. To be of maximum effectiveness in cohesive units, reward and punishment must be related to group norms. Both the action and the reward or punishment itself must be congruent with group norms. Material rewards and the ability to punish a soldier physically should also be available to the leader, but such devices must be viewed as complementary to reward and punishment through the group. In other words, reward and punishment must be related to the soldier's relationship with the group. The leader's ability to focus group pressures and acceptance or sanctioning of an individual is a source of tremendous power. It can threaten or heighten the soldier's sense of security, and source of affection and recognition, in such a manner that significant pressures become focused on the soldier to conform to group rules and procedures. In cohesive armies, awards and commendations as well as restriction and criticism are rooted strongly within the group and are implemented within full view of the unit.

Legitimate Power

Legitimate power in cohesive units may be defined as compliance with orders because of attitudes or beliefs that have their basis in a feeling of internalized "oughtness"—a sense of what is right and wrong that, in turn, is based on learned cultural values. Legitimate power tends to be the most impersonal source of power. It is dependent upon cultural value congruence among members of the unit and between leader and subordinates. Leader reliance on legitimate power is usually greater during the earlier period of a soldier's service or after defeat or extreme hardship when other sources of power are not as effective. In addition to arising from cultural values, legitimate power can also derive from the reputation of the organization the leader represents. For example, in Vietnam, an unknown US Army lieutenant tended to have more influence within the same unit than did an equally unknown Vietnamese lieutenant. Legitimate power reaches its most potent influence when the leader becomes a surrogate for authority figures held in greatest respect by unit members. Soldiers respond to legitimate power much in the same manner that citizens respond to a policeman or that a parishioner responds to a priest.

Referent Power

Referent power is most dependent on close, personal relationships between leaders and subordinate soldiers. Its great influence stems directly from the intense identification of the soldier with his immediate leader. Often, the leader approaches the stature of a loved and respected parent or of the charismatic leader who demonstrates consistently the Weberian quality of "grace," or the ability to consistently handle difficult situations well. Such referent power is based on the satisfaction of the soldier's personal needs for affection, recognition, and security through strong identification with a respected leader who has successfully led his unit through situations of danger and hardship. Leaders who maximize their referent power know the personal history and circumstances of all their subordinates. They know the aspirations, fears, capabilities, and attitudes of their soldiers in great detail and build relationships on these facts. In cohesive armies, the formation of such close ties between soldiers and leaders is not a matter of individual initiative or chance but of official policy.

Expert Power

Expert power may be defined as the soldier's compliance with a leader's orders because the leader is perceived as having superior knowledge and ability important to the soldier and his unit in the context of a current or expected situation. In hardship situations and in combat especially, leadership expertise that allows the leader to cope successfully with the situation is a significant source of power. The proven ability to carry out a tactical plan, to arrange for and adjust artillery, to demonstrate professional expertise with weapons, to navigate well, and to provide medical care and supplies are all significant sources of power. Just possessing information transmitted via radio, telephone, or messenger that is vital to the unit is a proven source of power. Armies desiring cohesive units must ensure that unit leaders are professionally trained and prepared. Leaders of front line units must be viewed as "men of steel" professionally equal to meeting all tasks demanded by the situation.

Leadership is probably the most important consideration in building cohesive units, and it requires extended and intensive face-to-face contact between leaders and soldiers. Leaders in cohesive units

1. are perceived by the group as professionally competent to meet successfully the situation and environment faced by the unit;

---

2. are not managerial in approach, but emphasize personal and continuing face-to-face contact with all soldiers in the leader's unit;

3. are found at the small-unit level, at squad, platoon, and company;

4. possess a degree of charisma (the ability to gracefully and repeatedly survive difficult situations) or act to neutralize the effects of failure. In either case the leader will use the perception of outside threat or difficult challenges to mobilize and coalesce the unit;

5. utilize the effects of indoctrination or civic education to maximize leadership influence;

6. emphasize, through professional ethics, that all members of the unit and especially the leaders share equally all hardship and danger;

7. are granted sufficient authority to control events or actions within the unit in order to meet their responsibility for building a cohesive unit;

8. will make use of all sources of power and influence within the group, including the power to reward, the power to coerce, legitimate power, referent power, and expert power.

CHAPTER VIII

Leadership in the North Vietnamese, US, Soviet, and Israeli Armies

Characteristics of North Vietnamese Leadership

THE NORTH VIETNAMESE SOLDIER generally had great confidence in his immediate leaders. He trusted them, respected their abilities, and generally believed that under their direction he and his fellow soldiers could successfully meet the situations and environment encountered by their unit.

Leadership in the North Vietnamese Army emphasized personal and continuing face-to-face contacts between leader and soldier. This relationship was the primary one in both the soldier and the leader's life, taking precedence over all others, and it was expected by each to continue to be such so long as both remained in the Army.

Recognizing that managerial and strategic skills are required at higher levels, leadership efforts in the North Vietnamese Army were focused at the military cell, squad, platoon, and company levels where the organization with its objectives is linked to the fighting soldier and his group by the leader. The North Vietnamese leader generally was very successful in dominating the primary group and controlling its operative group norms to ensure that the extraordinary cohesion that developed was congruent with North Vietnamese Army purposes.

Through demonstrated expertise and an extremely demanding, almost puritanical code of professional ethics that put the leader up front where he shared equally all hardship and danger, the North Vietnamese leader usually was able to lead his unit gracefully and repeatedly in surviving difficult situations. As a result, his personal reputation within his unit often approached some degree of charisma.

In those cases when he was not successful, he usually was able to rely on his expertise, formal and complete authority, and personal skills in manipulation of group pressures to neutralize the effects of failure or hardship and to use the perception of outside threat or difficult challenge to coalesce and control the unit.

Although the North Vietnamese desired to create "good communist soldiers," their attempts at indoctrination generally were not successful. Those soldiers who did respond, and were qualified otherwise (appropriate class background or skills), were recruited to be cadre-leaders. Vietnamese socialization did gain for the Army many of the effects sought through indoctrination and made leadership easier. Properly led, the Vietnamese soldier was more than willing to pursue the "honorable" task of defending Vietnam from foreigners and their "puppets."

The sources of the Vietnamese small-unit leader's personal influence within his unit were significant and were carefully nurtured through prescribed policies and through personal efforts.

Reward and Coercive Power

Reward power has been previously defined as the ability to exert influence in interpersonal relationships based upon the ability to reward. Likewise, coercive power is defined as influence whose basis is the ability to punish. Within the NVA, the cadre-leader did not have wide latitude to reward materially or to coerce individual soldiers. Resources for rewards, such as money or luxurious rest-and-recuperation vacations, were nonexistent. Similarly, physical punishment and incarceration were seldom relied upon. In extraordinary circumstances, a deviant soldier might be assigned to a "reeducation" camp for two to six months.

However, such an assignment was not perceived as imprisonment. Instead, as the name implies, the soldier was reeducated along the lines of "correct thought." Upon successful completion of his reeducation, he could, theoretically, rejoin a unit without bias.

As practiced within the NVA, reward and punishment were almost always related to the soldier's relationship with the primary group. The cadre's ability to regulate the group's acceptance or rejection of the individual was a source of tremendous power.

Among the most successful reward techniques were individual and unit awards and commendations. Through these awards, the individual was granted group recognition and esteem. Punishment was generally a group sanction entailing loss of face through a criticism session in which the violation of group or organizational discipline was publicly discussed, causing shame for the individual.

Rewards and punishment were always related to group norms. For example, a soldier criticized for being lazy might be cited as lacking in "commitment" or as guilty of "rightist thoughts" or "freedomism" (acting for one's own convenience), whereas an exemplary achievement might be cited as a commendable example of "correct thought," "virtue," and "revolutionary spirit."

The following excerpt from the minutes of a platoon party meeting illustrates how "Comrade Phuoc" was rewarded and how "Comrade Minh" was punished:

a. The . . . Group Chapter decided to have the shining example of Comrade Phuoc studied by the entire PRP Youth Group.

b. Comrade Minh was purged from the Group and put on probation for six months—if he made progress during this period he would be readmitted in the Group. He was disciplined for stealing two cans of rice from the unit, and for not observing the discipline of the unit. For example, he left the unit without permission, and when he was criticized by the collectivity he refused to admit his error.[1]

The NVA constantly shifted its organizational goals to meet the changing tactical situation. "Emulation" campaigns within the NVA ranks were designed to keep the soldier informed of the group's specific goals, providing a basis for measuring his contribution. From September 1966 through the autumn of 1967, for example, the NVA mounted a program entitled "Troop Training and Combat Competition—An Emulation Plan," designed to intensify its combat efforts against US forces. The program spelled out how NVA units could earn "good" or "fair" ratings. An NVA company was required to destroy one US platoon or two "puppet" (ARVN) platoons for a "good" rating or "annihilate two US squads or one puppet platoon" for a "fair" rating. In addition, "Heroic Aircraft Annihilator" and "Assault Hero" status were to be awarded to appropriate individuals. A private discussing this program stated that his squad leader

> killed 22 American soldiers in that battle and was elected "Valiant American Killer." He was also sent to attend the "Valiant American Killers Congress," 9 March 1966.[2]

Each soldier's performance in achieving group goals was routinely scrutinized by the cadre-leader. The following excerpt from an interview of a main force corporal describes how rewards and punishments were mediated through the group.

Question: Do you think that criticism and self-criticism is good or bad?

Answer: It is good. If there wasn't that system, the fighters' rank would immediately disintegrate. The criticism and self-criticism is a formidable weapon. I can tell you if there wasn't the criticism and self-criticism the fighters would all desert in one day. There was criticism and self-criticism every day. After a working day, a self-criticism session was immediately held at night. There were thirty nightly sessions a month. The criticism and self-criticism was part of the rules and regulations. It couldn't be missed. . . .

Question: What did the other men say? (about whether it was fair).

Answer: They also thought that the system was correct because it helped the cadres to make a difference between good and bad men. Those who had combat achievements or who did good work were commended, and those who had

shortcomings were criticized. This was
the guideline of the leadership.[3]

While a system of rewards and punishments is available to almost every army, the NVA related it to the group and refined it to
the point where it became a major motivational and control tech-
nique for reinforcing desired behavior and discouraging deviant
behavior.

Legitimate Power

The legitimate power of the NVA cadre-leader appeared to
rest on Vietnamese cultural values, which include fatalism, respect
for age, and nationalism. In addition, the fact that NVA cadre-
leaders were appointed by an organization that had achieved some
degree of legitimacy through its record of effective government in
North Vietnam and in certain areas of South Vietnam added to
their power.

In 1965, almost all men between the ages of 18 and 34 living
in areas controlled by the Vietcong were available for drafting
into the NVA.[4] The fatalistic draftee was likely to believe that he
was in the NVA through a process over which he had little control. He tended to respond to the situation with courage, patience,
and good will.

Leader reliance upon legitimate power, especially for controlling draftees, tended to be greater during the earlier period of
a soldier's service. Later, the bases of power shifted away from
legitimate power. Interviews of NVA draftees and volunteers with
long periods of service suggested that both had similar motivation
and that no distinction could be made in their motivation. Other
Vietnamese cultural values that contributed greatly toward cadre
legitimate power were respect and deference for elders. The trans-
ference of this respect to the NVA cadre was a common occurrence among NVA soldiers in their teens and twenties. In a very
real sense, the leader became a "respected elder" or surrogate
parent, fulfilling an important role. Numerous interviewees referred to the unit political officer in particular as the mother or
parent to the group, guiding and caring for it in every way.

Interviews with captured NVA soldiers indicate how cadre
authority was often interpreted in a parent-child context by the
fighters:

If the fighters said that the squad leader was harsh to them, he (the political officer) would explain to them that the squad leader had to be harsh because he wanted them to be good and respectable. He also reminded them that people often said, "When one loved his children, he gave them spankings, and when one hated his children, he let them play (a Vietnamese proverb)." To me, his explanation about the squad leader's behavior was very correct and very pleasing.[5]

The fact that the Vietcong were identified as fighting for Vietnamese independence also contributed to the leaders' legitimacy. As the successor to the Vietminh, who struggled against the French, many Vietnamese saw the NVA as merely the latest organization to take up the traditional banner of Vietnamese nationalism. One NVA prisoner stated:

I think that the people here support the Liberation Front because, in previous times, they had fought during the First Resistance against the French. They want Vietnam to be independent and reunified. They continue to support the Front because Vietnam is not yet independent and reunified.[6]

Finally, the mere fact that a cadre-leader holds a decision-making position in a legitimate organization such as the NVA means that individuals will respond to his direction in much the same manner that workmen respond to a foreman. Cadre-leaders appointed by a legitimate organization tend automatically to benefit from a halo effect, gaining legitimacy through association with that organization. A fighter pointed to one reason why NVA soldiers fought for the NVA:

They wanted their families to be honored by the Front and by the other villagers. For example, if there was a Front meeting in the village, those who had children in Front troops would be invited to sit in the front seats. The villagers liked to be honored that way.[7]

The NVA, like the Chinese Peoples Liberation Army before it, made great efforts to engender support from the people and gain legitimacy. An NVA soldier notes:

the men in the unit would always help the villagers at all types of work: for example, if the villagers were working on their land, or fishing, or digging ditches, building dams etc., we would come and give them a hand. Wherever and whenever we arrived we gave help to the people; they were thus very appreciative of our sincerity and loved us very much. Our motto is: The Army is welcomed wherever it goes, and loved wherever it stays. We will never touch even a piece of thread that belongs to the people. What belongs to the people remains theirs, and if by mistake it's damaged by us it will be compensated.[8]

Expert Power

The NVA recognized the importance of the cadre-leader being an expertly qualified person. As an agent of the party, the cadre-leader was required to be of high "ethical virtue." A second requisite was "talent" in military affairs, as a Vietnamese document indicates:

> To have an excellent cadre contingent serving as the nucleus of the armed forces, the Party set forth an ethical and talent criteria. . . . Morality and ability are two fundamental qualities that all our officers must have. He who lacks one of these qualities cannot become an officer. President Ho taught us "He who has talents must have virtues. He who has talents, but has no virtues . . . does harm to the country. He who has virtues, but no talents resembles a Buddha who, staying in the pagoda, does nobody any good." [9]

Evidence is plentiful that NVA soldiers saw their cadre-leaders as "men-of-steel," capable of expertly performing, for the benefit of the group, all tasks demanded by the situation. The following excerpts illustrate the soldiers' respect for the cadre. One soldier who was also a junior leader stated:

> All of them [the cadre] had been trained in specialized schools, and matured in actual combat. Therefore all of them were worthy of confidence and admiration. Of course I had confidence in them. I could see they were men of good experience; I felt proud of them.

In large part, he saw the leader's influence with the fighters as dependent upon the leader's performance in combat. A cadre noted:

> I also participated in direct combat side-by-side with the fighters. You see, the thing was, if you were a good fighter, then you would be listened to by others, moreover, if you treated others well, and if you were a good fighter also, then your work as a political cadre was already half over. A political cadre should be the one who acts first and then speaks.[10]

Successful decisions reflecting expertise also contributed to cadre influence. Another soldier observed:

I as well as other men had much confidence in the commanding cadres . . . because they were very clear-sighted. For example, the commanding cadres ordered the unit to move to
another place just a day or half-day before the old campsite
was bombarded by aircraft and artillery. This made the men
have confidence in the cadre.[11]

When heavy cadre casualties required the rapid creation of
new leaders, temporary lack of expertise reduced cadre influence
among the fighters.[12] A private whose unit suffered heavy cadre
losses points to a common feeling among fighters who saw their
cadre as basically unable to lead the group effectively:

Because of heavy losses, most of the company, platoon, and
squad leaders were new replacements. . . . The new cadres
weren't as good as the earlier ones. They didn't know much
about strategy and had no experience in tactics. In the last
months, many fighters showed no respect and less obedience
to platoon and squad leaders because most of those people
didn't deserve the appointment and were not up to their
tasks.[13]

Referent Power

In many cases, the most potent source of cadre power was the
intense identification of NVA soldiers with their cadre-leaders.
Sometimes the cadre-leader approached the status of the charismatic leader who had demonstrated the Weberian quality of grace
in difficult situations and was expected to do so in the future.

Referent power, derived from the satisfaction gained by the
soldier through personal identification with the leader, overlaps
other sources of power. For example, reward and expert power
contribute to the desire to identify with the cadre-leader. The
formation of close identities between the men and the cadre was
not left to chance within the NVA. It was official policy that such
relationships be developed to their fullest. Leaders were repeatedly told:

We must train ourselves into simple, modest, diligent, thrifty,
honest, selfless, upright, and impartial cadres; resolutely
eradicate individualism; and insure that in construction and
combat and under favorable or difficult circumstances, a correct attitude is constantly maintained toward the enemy, the
Party, the people, and our comrades and comrades-in-arms in
combat, in work performance, and in other activities.[14]

A prisoner's remark is representative of how the cadre went about establishing close ties with their men:

> As far as relations between the Leaders and the fighters were concerned, I can also say that close ties existed between them. Take, for example, the case of some of the fighters becoming ill: often a cadre would take care of the sick fighters. There were also cases of cadres sharing their food and clothing rations with the fighters. I can tell you that we cadres shared everything with our fighters. There was no case of each one keeping his own possession to himself alone, or hiding it away from others. The friendship and unity that existed among the cadres and fighters were as close as among the cadres themselves.[15]

The results of such cadre efforts usually produced attitudes similar to those expressed by a private, first class, discussing one of his cadre-leaders:

> He was the best educated man in the unit. In any circumstance he always succeeded in producing reasonable arguments. So he won the mind of any person he had to deal with. He was honest and impartial.[16]

A portion from another POW interview gives a more comprehensive picture of fighter identity with their cadre:

> *Question*: Describe the cadres in your unit. What kind of persons were they?
>
> *Answer*: All of the cadres, platoon cadres and company cadres were very nice people. They were well-trained and well-educated. I heard that they were people who formerly had fought against the French.
>
> *Question*: What did you think of them?
>
> *Answer*: . . . . We all respected and obeyed our leaders because, as I told you, they were nice people. They never did anything to hurt the feelings of the men in the unit. They always lived with us, ate with us, and they understood us very well. We strictly obeyed any order received from them. . . .
>
> *Question*: Do you think the political cadre knew everything that was going on in the unit?

Answer: He lived with, and ate with us. Some-
                 times, when we talked to each other, he
                 came and talked to us too. I think he
                 knew everything.[17]

The role of the unit political officer in particular was important in the maintenance of close cadre-fighter relationships,
especially during the hardships and dangers of sustained combat.
Another excerpt from an NVA rallier interview illustrates the importance of the cadre-leader's role, the identity need he satisfied
for the fighters, and the disintegrative effect when this need was
not met:

Question: Who was in charge of . . . morale prob-
                 lems in your unit?

Answer: My unit had an excellent political cadre.
                 He was very skillful in convincing people,
                 particularly those who worried about
                 their families. He used to get in contact
                 with the soldiers in private to advise and
                 comfort them. Everyone liked him and
                 followed his advice. Unfortunately he
                 was transferred to another place, leaving
                 the post vacant for two months. If he had
                 remained longer in my unit, I would have
                 been unable to leave. . . .

Question: Did the political cadre in your unit do his
                 work well?

Answer: The political cadre in my unit performed
                 his duties perfectly well. Every soldier ap-
                 preciated and obeyed him. He was very
                 useful to the unit in settling conflicts and
                 in raising the fighters' morale. They
                 strengthened discipline and prevented
                 desertion. Only during his absence from
                 the unit did many desertions occur, mine
                 included. I think if he left the unit for five
                 or six months without a good replace-
                 ment, most of the people would
                 desert . . . his behavior, attitudes and
                 performance always remained the same.
                 He never lost the heart of any soldier.[18]

Characteristics of US Leadership

To the limited degree that today's US soldier thinks about it, he probably sees his immediate leadership as professionally competent to lead his unit successfully in combat. Small-unit leaders, especially junior officers, are exposed to the finest courses of instruction offered in any army. When they graduate from these courses, they are among the most expert small-unit leaders in the world. A demanding code of professional ethics requires that US leaders lead by example and share equally all hardships and danger. Yet small-unit leaders are finding it difficult to grasp control of their units and create the cohesive units required to win in combat. The reason is not the result of major shortcomings in their expertise, leadership abilities, or desire. Rather, it is the result of a series of decisions, made primarily within the past two decades, that tend to separate the small-unit leader (NCO and officer) from his soldiers. These decisions have moved the US Army away from traditional and proven policies towards those designed to make a volunteer Army more palatable to the public and to potential recruits.

Another very significant part of this trend is that there appear to be noticeably fewer squad leaders, platoon sergeants, and first sergeants of the type once referred to as the "backbone of the Army." These NCOs were broadly representative of American society, they knew their jobs better than anyone else, they loved their troops, and they expected to be with them indefinitely. Large portions of the NCO corps are turning away from this traditional concept and from the career pattern of squad leader, platoon sergeant, and perhaps first sergeant. So many NCOs are avoiding the traditional career path that only a little more than one-half of the Army's first sergeant positions are filled by NCOs in the grade of E-8. The Army's response has been to offer monetary incentives rather than to question why senior NCOs are pursuing patterns other than the traditional one. In this regard, one notes that recent sergeants major promotion boards have selected as many administrative career E-8s as infantry E-8s for promotion to E-9. Personal observations as a battalion commander support this trend. Large numbers of combat arms NCOs actively seek administrative positions through special duty, MOS (military occupational specialty) change, or taking advantage of physical profiles while squad and platoon sergeant positions in line units are left unfilled or viewed as temporary jobs until an administrative position opens up.

Central to this trend is what many observers would identify as the ascendency during the past 20 years of a managerial approach to decisionmaking. Basic organizational assumptions about how to motivate soldiers have significantly affected the leader's ability to influence their behavior. This approach assumes that the soldier is an economic man motivated primarily by personal gain. To entice soldiers to do the tough jobs such as serve in the combat arms, utilitarian motivation appears to be the answer. The higher pay necessary to compete for "labor" in the market has had the effect of making soldiering much more of an occupation. The Army has had to adopt many of the attractions offered by business in order to compete. As Charles Moskos has pointed out, the achievement of recruiting goals is the major criteria of success for the volunteer Army. Cohesion and leadership, being essentially immeasurable, are considered to be comparatively insignificant.

One of the most significant changes of the volunteer Army has been the high pay given lower-ranking enlisted men. Along with associated policies (such as relaxation of pass policies), higher pay has permitted junior enlisted men much more independence. The majority of soldiers now spend most of their time away from the unit. The squad leader and platoon sergeant have become "shift bosses" controlling their soldiers approximately eight hours a day.

Combined with a series of court decisions that significantly shifted priorities toward safeguarding the rights of the individual and away from traditional practices designed to create group discipline and cohesion, the effects of the move toward the occupational model of an army have had profound effects on the abilities of American leaders to create cohesive units.

The sources of power the small-unit leader requires to influence his soldiers have unintentionally been weakened to the point that it is not possible to create the degree of cohesion seen in other armies. If the ultimate purpose has been to create an army that pleases almost everyone, the US Army has done that. The soldiers are happy with their pay in a job that isn't too demanding and that requires little sacrifice; the public is happy because most don't have the inconvenience of serving; and the nation's elected officials are happy because most of their constituents are pleased. Unfortunately, this state of affairs has been brought about through a set of policies that, while enticing enough volunteers, has made the human element of the US Army less important than it is in other top armies in the world today. As a result, the United States no longer has a tough, professional army that matches other leading armies in an essential element of combat power—cohesion.

Efforts to correct the situation have been directed at a level much too high within the organization. While extended command tours at battalion and brigade level and conversion to a regimental-style system will help, these efforts neglect to put priority at lower levels where cohesion is created. Cohesion occurs primarily at the squad, platoon, and company levels; it is created primarily by sergeants and junior officers exercising leadership through a stable, long-term relationship with their soldiers. To build a cohesive army, leadership skills in company and lower-level units, which are the most crucial, must be given priority.

In Vietnam, for example, the Vietcong recognized the importance of this concept. If a platoon or squad leader became a casualty and there was no fully qualified individual available within the unit to take his place, a fully qualified officer from a higher level was sent to lead that unit permanently. Within the US Army, this is not the practice. Acting sergeants are routinely appointed. While the best man available is usually appointed, little thought is given to the individual's overall ability and almost never is a senior noncommissioned officer sent "down" from the staff to lead the lacking platoon or squad. Perhaps the fault is systemic, resting in the fact that recent US Army leadership efforts have been focused at battalion and brigade levels, where extensive efforts have been made to appoint selected leaders for extended tours. While these efforts may do some good, they miss the mark. As noted, cohesive armies are built primarily at squad and platoon levels; hence, an army must place its leadership efforts there.

The possibility of significant bias in the current emphasis on battalion and brigade leadership must be recognized. The fact that most Pentagon action officers in the US Army working on these questions are lieutenant colonels and colonels who tend to project their rank into organizational solutions should not be overlooked. As a result, battalion and brigade command positions are emphasized. If the action officers determining US Army policy in these areas were senior sergeants and company grade officers, the proposed solutions would more likely be at platoon and company levels and would further cohesion in the US Army.

The sources of influence required by a leader in order to create a cohesive unit are potent and varied. Unfortunately, the small-unit leader in today's US Army does not have full access to these necessary sources of leadership power.

Expert Power

The extensive training received by US small-unit leaders places them among the most competent military leaders worldwide. Through a system of progressive branch and specialty schools and courses, lieutenants and captains as well as squad and platoon sergeants learn skills that enable them to meet successfully all anticipated situations in combat. In past wars, a leader's ability to care for his troops by calling in defensive air and artillery strikes and by arranging for resupply and medical evacuation was, along with his tactical skills, an important source of personal influence within his unit. If he were perceived as being the most expert in these skills, his influence and ability to lead were greatly enhanced. Expert power, however, is most potent in combat or extended training situations when these skills are of greater importance to unit success and survival. In peacetime and short-term training situations and in a civilian milieu where American soldiers spend most of their time, the need for military expertise is minimal, and therefore the personal expertise of the leader is less useful in building cohesion. If the American soldier spent significantly more of his time within the environs of his unit, as soldiers in other armies do, expert power would become a much greater source of influence for the leader.

Reward and Coercive Power

The power to reward and punish are not significant sources of power for the American small-unit leader. For maximum effectiveness in a small unit, reward and punishment must be related to dominant group norms within the unit, and the leader must be in control of using these norms in order to control soldier behavior. This is not the case in the US Army, except in elite units. The American soldier's bonds to his unit are generally so tenuous that group pressures within the unit play little role in influencing his behavior. The soldier's primary social affiliations are outside the unit with groups the leader has little chance of influencing. The inability to reward or punish the soldier through his need for peer esteem and recognition is a significant loss of influence for the leader.

Other means of rewarding the soldier through symbolic acts, such as handing him pay on payday, have also been removed from the purview of the small-unit leader. The inability of the squad leader, platoon sergeant, or platoon leader to control his soldiers 24 hours a day has made irrelevant what has traditionally been one of the greatest sources of influence possible at that level—The Pass. Further, the inability to maintain discipline in his own right, through extra duty and other such restrictions, has removed another significant source of influence from the company-grade leader. Promotions are largely seen as being independent of the soldier's immediate squad or platoon and more dependent upon centralized board proceedings. Soldiers perceive it as their right to appear before the promotion board so long as they meet the basic criteria, which are established largely independently of the squad and platoon leaders. Although these leaders have a veto over soldier promotions, the exercise of this veto prerogative is often seen as a negative influence on soldier morale rather than as a positive source of influence for the unit leader.

Perhaps most significantly, the prerogative of the Army to enforce rules necessary for discipline and cohesion has been significantly weakened by the court system. Over the past 15 years, the Court of Military Appeals, the Federal Appellate Courts, and the Supreme Court have turned away from a prior principle that held, in accordance with democratic tradition, that soldiers give up some of their individual rights while they serve. The commander was given the primary responsibility for rule enforcement under a code that gave priority to creating and maintaining military discipline. Under this system the priorities were clear, the rules were explained, and their enforcement was fair and swift. What has emerged from the highest courts over the past 15 years is a series of new precedents that have given priority to applying all legal safeguards and rights applicable to civilians and individual soldiers. The individual and his rights now have priority over the welfare of the unit. The maintenance of discipline and cohesion has suffered significantly as a result.[19] Civilian contract law is now applied to conditions of a soldier's service; a unit commander cannot personally conduct a search of his unit for any purpose and then press charges against soldiers found in violation of law, such as drug or weapons possession. Reinforcing the notion that military service can be compartmentalized into an eight-hour day and that the soldier is a civilian for the remainder of the day, the Supreme Court has ruled that the Army does not have courts-martial jurisdiction over a soldier off duty or off post.[20] Soldiers are allowed to bring suit against commanders attempting to maintain discipline (such as a suit against the Army urinalysis program to detect drug abuse). These and other such rulings recast many of the traditional practices considered necessary to maintain discipline and build cohesion.

Legitimate Power

A small-unit leader's legitimate power is directly related to the perceived status of the Army in American society. In other words, operative legitimate power means that the soldier believes he "ought" to be in the Army and obey Army officials because he has learned that it is the responsibility of a citizen to serve in defense of the nation.

This learned cultural value is not uniform in the United States. America's fractured consensus about the citizen's proper duties with regard to serving in defense of his country was described previously. For the reasons cited in chapter 6, legitimate power based on a strong military ethos in American society is a very weak source of influence for the small-unit leader. More and more, he is being forced to turn to a different sort of legitimate, but much less potent, power—that found in the relationship between employer and employee. This type of motivation is well-established in American society. It is the motivation of the marketplace and assumes the soldier is an economic man and thus can be influenced through utilitarian means. While marketplace motivation is legitimate, it is weak. It casts the soldier in the role of employee with the possibility of "opting out," if the going gets too tough. In an Army where a primary source of leader influence is marketplace motivation, the bond of a soldier to his unit and his leader is not very strong.

Referent Power

By far the strongest influence available to any leader is referent power. History is replete with battles won through the endurance and capabilities of cohesive armies formed primarily on the basis of referent power. Referent power is dependent upon the identity between leader and soldier formed through close, frequent, and structured association. Both parties expect the relationship to endure for an extended period. In such a relationship, the leader knows the personal history, background, aspirations, fears, capabilities, and attitudes of his soldier and uses these facts to promote the soldier's identity with him and the unit—a unit that becomes the primary social affiliation for all assigned soldiers and that is bonded together to the degree that the soldier's and the leader's expectations about the soldier's personal behavior are the same.

To a large degree, internal organizations and current US Army practices and policies deny referent power to small-unit leaders. The cumulative effects of the occupational model of the Army previously described prevent the frequent, structured, personal, and relatively permanent association between small-unit leaders and soldiers necessary for referent power to become operative and for cohesion to emerge. Very high pay for junior enlisted personnel, permanent-pass and liberal "out" policies, persistent personnel turbulence, primary affiliation with "outside" groups often on basis of race, drugs, or sex, large numbers of married soldiers, significant numbers of singles maintaining a room in the barracks but living off post, judicial erosion of company-grade leaders' authority, soldiers' perceptions of their role as a job rather than as a vocation, configuration of rooms, mess halls, and other facilities, and other similar factors combine to ensure that the small unit remains a fragmented group, largely unable to coalesce around its leaders and produce cohesion to the degree it is achieved in other armies.

Characteristics of Soviet Leadership

Unlike most other armies, the Soviet officer corps, not the NCO corps, is the backbone of the Soviet Army.[21] Soviet officers perform many of the important training and supervisory functions traditionally performed by sergeants. Combined with the ethnic, boredom, drinking, and other problems described earlier, not having a strong NCO corps presents major leadership problems to the Soviet Army for two reasons. First, leadership efforts are not focused at the small-unit level, especially at the squad and platoon levels. Because there are often not enough experienced officers available and because NCO experience and quality at these levels is generally low, the Soviet Army is not well represented at the level where an organization's best leaders are necessary if cohesive units are to be created.[22] Second, although the Soviet officer corps is perceived to be extremely competent, adhering to a demanding code of professional ethics, it includes within its ethos an elitist attitude that in many respects makes it an extremely privileged class, one that emphasizes material benefits and the prerogatives of rank and position. As a result, the most competent leadership within the Soviet Army, the officer corps, is effectively separated from the soldiers of the Soviet Army. The extended, frequent, and purposeful face-to-face contacts between leader and soldier necessary to build cohesive units generally are not present in most Soviet Army units. The Soviets have officially recognized the importance of the close leader-soldier relationships necessary to build cohesion and are attempting to improve the situation.[23] They have recently created the rank of warrant officer to bridge the gap between officer and NCO and are taking other measures to improve the quality of NCOs.

The Soviets deride the excessive reliance the United States puts on initiative (translated in Russian as "native wit"). They maintain that the biggest obstacle to combat effectiveness is stress on the individual soldier caused by the surprise, fear, and hardship found in combat.[24] Instead of relying on the initiative, the Soviets place heavy emphasis on carefully worked out and detailed plans, characterized by surprise and maneuver, often without the complete massing of forces needed in order to achieve surprise. To enable the Soviet soldier to withstand the effects of stress, the Soviet Army emphasizes (1) unit cohesion under reliable leaders; (2) training under combat conditions, or practicing to be miserable (they believe that a certain amount of conditioning to stress is possible and expect that pre-conditioned soldiers will be better able to resist the fear and hardship of combat); and (3) drill in training. The Soviets believe that the first casualty of stress will be "clear and reasoned thinking." The last thing to go from a soldier's mind will be "well-rehearsed drills." Therefore, drill and repetition will eventually win out over intellect, wit, and initiative.[25] In essence, the Soviets believe that well-drilled units, formed into cohesive Kollectives, under the control of reliable leaders, following detailed plans, will prove superior in future wars. They believe their doctrine is based on years of wisdom and accumulated knowledge gained through surviving an intensity of warfare in World War II experienced by few other armies.

The Soviets further believe that they have a reliable Army because of the broad and powerful effects of Russian socialization, which gives enormous legitimacy to the Soviet Army and creates the expectation that all Soviet citizens have concerning their responsibilities toward serving the Army and the State. The Soviet soldier expects the intense supervision, indoctrination, regimentation, and hardship to which he is exposed. The resulting boredom, drinking, and occasional insubordination are not viewed as subversive but almost as normal elements of the milieu, as the Soviet soldier attempts to cope with a two-to-three-year enlistment that is purposefully made difficult and stressful by Soviet officers as part of their philosophy of training. Added to the legitimizing effects of socialization is an extremely exacting and comprehensive set of military regulations that prescribes correct actions and behavior for almost all envisioned circumstances. The authority of the Soviet officer to enforce regulations and orders is complete. In certain circumstances, he even has authority for on-the-spot executions. As might be expected, willingness to deviate from prescribed procedures to exercise individual initiative is rare. There is a strong institutional bias toward protecting oneself from failure. If prescribed procedures have been followed and failure occurs, individuals cannot be held responsible. The Soviets recognize the need for some leadership initiative [26] and yet appear to be unable to nurture it sufficiently because of the continuing demands for exacting discipline and careful adherence to set plans and procedures. In short, the bases for Soviet Army leaders' influence over their soldiers are mixed.

Reward and Coercive Power

Detailed regulations listing all undesired behavior and appropriate punishments are widely distributed within the Soviet Army.[27] Military tribunals impose courts-martial sentences that are often served in disciplinary battalions. For less serious offenses within units, commanders at various levels have authority to take a number of actions. A tank commander, for example, can impose punishment on the tank driver even if both are of the same rank.[28] Small-unit commanders can also mete out rewards. Typical rewards are

> a statement of gratitude orally or in the form of a written order, removal of punishment imposed earlier, awarding of certificates, bestowing of valuable gifts or money, and awarding of the chest badge for an outstanding soldier. Disciplinary punishment includes admonition, reprimand, strict reprimand, arrest with detention in the guardhouse for a period of ten days, deprivation of the chest badge of outstanding soldier, removal from the post, discharge into the reserve until the expiration of the service period, and deprivation of military rank.[29]

While a formal system of punishment exists, it appears that commanders are reluctant to use it extensively. Because of the intense competition among units, many commanders attempt to keep punishment statistics at a low level, thus indicating a lack of significant disciplinary problems.[30] As a substitute, commanders often rely on informal group punishments such as harsh training to bring pressures within the group to punish and correct individual offenses.[31]

Even rewards, such as highly prized time away from the unit, do not always fully benefit the unit leader. Suvorov notes:

> On Sundays, the commander of a sub-unit is allowed to send 10% of his NCOs and soldiers into town during daylight hours. This might seem to be a way of encouraging those who deserve it. In fact, however, although he may make a soldier a present of eight hours in this way, he cannot be sure that his battalion or regimental commander will not overrule him by stopping all leave. Besides, platoon and company commanders themselves are not enthusiastic about letting soldiers out of camp. If a soldier is checked by a patrol in the town and they find the slightest thing wrong, the officer who allowed the soldier to leave his barracks is held responsible. A commander, therefore, prefers to send soldiers off for the day in a group, under the eye of the political officer. This is the only way in which Soviet soldiers are allowed to go into a town in Eastern Europe and it is very frequently used in the Soviet Union, too. Since a Soviet soldier does not like being part of a convoy, he just does not bother to leave camp.[32]

Significantly, the small-unit commander, through team, squad, platoon, and higher levels, has authority to reward and punish based upon the functional authority of his position. He does not have to request delayed action from authorities at higher levels. The impact of his decision to reward or punish, especially informally, is immediate and recognized as a prerogative of his position.

The Soviet Army recognizes the power of the Kollective to reward and punish in pursuit of Army goals. Soviet military texts on military psychology give instructions to leaders on how to control opinion formulation within the group to ensure that peer pressures are focused on a deviant soldier to isolate him from the group and then bring him back into the group on the leader's terms.[33] The Soviet Army recognizes the strong influence available to a unit leader through dispensing rewards and punishment via group pressures and is taking steps to reinforce this method of control. Results, however, appear to be mixed. Success has been limited because junior NCOs are not well established within their units as leaders capable of bringing about congruence between group and organizational needs. It appears that Soviet Army NCOs at lower unit levels are too inexperienced and generally identify with the soldiers at the expense of Army goals. An official Soviet Army publication discusses the situation:

> In contrast to officers, sergeants (senior NCOs) are not signif-
> icantly older than their subordinates, and hence they have
> little advantage in experience which is an important factor in
> the moral and psychological influence upon people. Also, for
> completely understandable reasons, sergeants (senior NCOs)
> can only slightly surpass their subordinates in service experi-
> ence . . . and are not always able to find a correct approach
> to the men or rationally use their disciplinary rights. . . .
> They are also more susceptible to the influence of the soldier's
> opinion than are officers. All this makes it difficult for ser-
> geants to establish authority as the moral and psychological
> basis for proper relations with soldiers.[34]

Expert Power

The Soviet Army recognizes that expert power is a significant
source of influence for leaders. High Soviet authorities stress that
the leader must strive to "be respected not only as a lieutenant or
captain but as an expert in his job . . . he should win authority,
and win it primarily by knowledge and experience." [35] To become
well prepared, junior and warrant officers spend up to four or five
years in one or more of approximately 140 specialized military
schools. Soldiers under their command are well guided and appear
to have confidence in the ability of these leaders.[36]

Two significant factors appear to work against the expert
junior leader's ability to influence his soldiers. One is the obvious
undermining of the junior leader's professional status by less well-
qualified political officers. It is obvious to the Soviet soldier, as
Scott and Scott point out, that the Party attaches "greater importance to the political than to the military qualifications of
officers." [37] Because Soviet Army political officers enter the military through special academies and have relatively fewer military
skills than regular officers, they tend to be somewhat isolated
within the officer corps. Unlike the North Vietnamese political officer, who is foremost a military leader, the Soviet political officer
is not perceived to be a military expert and his authority over military experts is resented. Second, while Soviet leaders are well
qualified for their duties, they are narrowly focused; hence, they
can quickly "get out of their area" of expertise merely by being

put in a situation that changes their duties even slightly. As long as operations proceed according to a set plan, the Soviet leader's expertise will tend to be a source of power in influencing his soldiers. But the lack of initiative evident at all levels of command below the General Staff level is a distinct liability. Because of the risk of failure and the need to assess blame, initiative is discouraged and usually penalized within the Soviet Army. In a turbulent situation where pre-established plans have been discarded and communication with higher headquarters is not possible, most Soviet leaders would "be at a loss." [38] The obvious lack of leadership expertise or willingness to improvise in such situations presents major problems for Soviet leaders attempting to influence their soldiers.

Legitimate Power

The entire socialization process within Soviet society appears to reinforce the legitimate power of Soviet Army leaders. Soviet citizens have a strong need for direction and control by recognized authority as a result of learned cultural values. Within the Soviet Army this need for direction is translated into a strong sense of complying with orders merely because they are issued by formal authority figures. From an egalitarian beginning that did away with all rank distinctions after the Revolution of 1917, the Soviet Army has gradually instituted a system of rank, prerogatives, and privileges that requires compliance with a well-developed set of regulations and procedures; these require the soldiers' compliance on the basis of formal authority alone.[39]

Legitimate power appears to be the primary source of leader influence, even though top Soviet leadership recognizes that referent power is probably the most powerful form of leader influence and would like to maximize this source of leader power.

Referent Power

The solidarity of the Kollective under the positive influence of Soviet leaders is the desired goal within all units of the Soviet Army. While major problems prevent the accomplishment of this goal in the near term, the Soviet Army has instituted policies promoting such leadership practices and is actively working toward achieving this goal.

Official Soviet guidance to officers in the field recognizes the power of the Kollective when under the positive control of its leaders and emphasizes the need to develop trust and mutual loyalty between leaders and soldiers necessary for referent power. Only when the soldier believes that his immediate leader has that soldier's welfare in mind and demonstrates the capability of successfully leading the Kollective through difficult hardships and danger will that soldier identify strongly with the leader and permit him to exercise influence over his own behavior.

The Soviets realize that the key to referent power is leader control of the group and the formation of group norms that are congruent with Soviet Army objectives. Goldhamer notes:

> Soviet writings on morale, solidarity, and discipline increasingly emphasize the importance of a knowledge of psychology and sociology for understanding and motivating soldiers. Company officers, particularly the company political officers, study the character, behavior, and attitudes of the men.[40]

Official Soviet texts on "Control of Collective Attitudes" also emphasize the point:

> The various meetings of personnel are the chief means of expressing a collective opinion, and at the same time a method for shaping it. . . . The opinion of a meeting of personnel, as a rule, has a very strong effect upon the men. This must be used carefully and skillfully in endeavoring to use group opinion for solving fundamental issues. . . . [41]

The Soviets are aware of the power a leader can achieve when the group identifies with him and, as noted above, are also aware of the control techniques necessary to achieve this power. But they have not yet taken the major reforms necessary to modify the exacting discipline and severe daily regimen that is the primary control system in use within the Soviet Army today.[42] Other significant changes would also be necessary. The Soviet officer corps emphasizes traditions, adopted from the Tzarist Imperial Army, that effectively separate it from close contact with the Soviet soldiers. Though tactically sound and possessing great expertise, the Soviet officer is not disposed to promote the close professional relationships with soldiers that other armies have successfully formed in creating an enormously powerful source of influence for small-unit leaders. Soviet Army NCOs as presently trained and assigned are also not capable of forming militarily cohesive units. As noted earlier, most are assigned for two years only, are usually of the same age and general experience as the soldiers they are to lead, and usually perceive themselves as just another soldier with little difference in status. Because they eat, sleep, and work with their units to an extreme, they identify primarily with their soldiers, rather than with Army objectives.[43] Shelyag, Glotochkin, and Platonov illustrate the limitations and basic qualifications of Soviet NCOs:

> The training divisions have no fixed establishment of personnel: every six months each division receives ten thousand recruits to train. After five months of brutally tough training these trainees become sergeants and are sent to combat divisions, to replace those who have been demobilized. Then the training division receives another ten thousand and the cycle begins again. Thus each training division turns out twenty thousand sergeants a year. Each trainee spends half of his first year at the training division, is promoted and then spends the remaining eighteen months of his service with a combat division.[44]

The type of training and the leadership example set for NCO trainees within NCO training divisions help explain why Soviet sergeants are not the backbone of the Soviet Army. Suvorov observes:

> In a training division, a sergeant simply dominates his trainees, totally ignoring any views they may have. In addition, each platoon commander in a training division, supervising thirty or forty young trainees, is allowed to retain the services of one or two of the toughest of them. A sergeant in a training division also knows that he would have nothing like the same authority in a combat division. While he is still a trainee, therefore, he picks noisy quarrels with his fellows, in the hope that his platoon commander will notice and decide that he is someone who should be kept on to join the staff after the end of the course. He cannot afford to reduce his aggressiveness if he succeeds in landing a job with the training division, or he may find himself sent off to join a combat division, having been replaced by some young terror who is only too ready to spend all his nights as well as his days

enforcing order and discipline. (If, however, this should happen, he would soon realize that he is unlikely to be sent on anywhere else from a combat division and that he can therefore afford to let up a bit and to slacken the reins.)

Discipline in a training division is almost unbelievably strict. If you have not experienced life in one you could never imagine what it is like. For instance, you might have a section of non-smokers headed by a sergeant who does smoke. Every member of the section will carry cigarettes and matches in his pocket. If the sergeant, apparently without realizing that he is doing so, lifts two fingers to his mouth, the section will assume that he is in need of a cigarette. As one, ten trainees will rush forward, pulling cigarette packets from their pockets. The sergeant hesitates, considering which of the ten stands highest in his favour at that moment, and finally selects one of the cigarettes he is offered. By doing so, he rewards a trainee for his recent performance.

Older and more senior NCOs tend to follow the officer example and isolate themselves from the individual soldier except for formal contacts based upon extremely strict discipline.[45]

The unrelenting requirements of the daily training regimen in all Soviet Army combat units drive everyone—officers, NCOs, and soldiers alike—with their demands and competition. Along with the other divisive factors described earlier (such as the problems of ethnic conflict, apathy, and drinking), the tough daily requirements do not allow leaders the time or initiative necessary to break out of the present system toward a more positive leadership approach.[46]

Characteristics of Israeli Leadership

Israelis have always stated that their security problem is unlike that of any other country. They are unique in that they have had to struggle as a nation for physical survival since 1948. During the course of four major wars and continuous smaller conflicts since that time, Israel's strategy of conducting brief but intensive warfare to defeat its enemies decisively has produced military leaders of the highest quality. Not only the highly visible top-ranking leadership but especially the lowest-ranking leadership at squad and platoon levels was exemplary. During the Sinai Campaign and the Six-Day War, about 50 percent of all Israeli

casualties were officers.[47] The character of Israeli leadership reflects the Israeli belief that the Israeli Defense Forces (IDF) are
"as good as [their] officers":

> Every officer was in the thick of it. Platoon commanders and
> brigadiers . . . knew their jobs well, had unlimited drive and
> determination, were keen, quick-thinking, and imbued with
> the aggressive spirit. Above all, they were offensive-minded
> and held an insatiable will to win. . . .[48]

While the strategic skills of Israel's top military leadership
have led to impressive victories, almost all of those within the IDF
recognize that the key element in these victories is the Israeli soldier and his immediate leadership at squad, crew, and platoon
levels. To an exceedingly high degree, there is almost complete
congruence within these units between the goals and behavior of
individual soldiers and the objectives of the organization. Because
Israeli procedures for recruiting junior officers and NCOs ensure
that the most qualified are selected for leadership positions, Army
leaders are generally very successful in dominating the primary
groups within the Israeli Army. As a result, the IDF is able to
achieve a high degree of military cohesion which allows leaders at
lower levels the initiative to explore opportunities in combat that
few other armies are able to achieve:

> Since the approved style of combat leadership is based on per-
> sonal example, problem-solving and "leadership" contact,
> knowing that he will be able to "pull" his men after him by
> being the first to advance, the officer can choose daring
> tactical solutions which he might otherwise have to reject.
> When "leadership" consists of ordering reluctant men to ad-
> vance bold tactics are out of the question. . . .[49]

The extraordinary action of the Israeli soldier in combat is
based on the almost absolute control of the group over his behavior. Men said that what worried them most during combat was
what others would think of them. Within the small unit the pre-
eminence of the leader is assured because he sets the example in all
those areas held in highest value by the group. Generally unsur-
passed in military expertise, the Israeli leader adheres to a
spartan, almost puritanical code of professional conduct, which
eschews monetary gain and special status but offers recognized
stature within the group as the primary reward.[50]

Within the Israeli Army, a system of employing "military psychologists" to conduct morale surveys on a regular basis has determined that several major factors affect the morale of Israeli troops. These factors have been confirmed most recently in IDF actions in Lebanon, where troop surveys found a very significant statistical correlation between (1) unit cohesion and perceived high levels of morale within the company, (2) confidence in leaders at company and lower unit levels, and (3) the individual soldier's confidence in himself as a soldier.[51]

Reward and Coercive Power

Very little of the Israeli leader's influence over his troops is based on his perceived ability to reward or punish in a concrete manner. The Israelis have rejected motivating soldiers through higher pay or other incentives as being basically flawed. Likewise, physical restraint or coercion play a small role in Israeli leadership techniques. This slight use of physical punishment is even true for the limited number of soldiers with criminal or deviant behavior records drafted each year in an attempt to reform them for Israeli society.

Within the IDF, reward and punishment are usually related to the individual soldier's relationship with the primary group or unit. The leader's ability to control group sanctions and therefore the behavior of the individual soldier is an enormous source of personal power.

The decisive role of social ties and comradeship and the opportunity it presents to the leader to grant recognition and build the individual soldier's esteem in the eyes of the group are perhaps the most potent source of reward available to the Israeli leader.[52] Informal verbal approval is the most common form of recognition. Next are the many informal letters of commendation and appreciation through which the unit leader extends recognition. Such letters are the frequent form of recognition and reward; because they are not lightly given, they are accepted within the group as being deserved praise for a job well done.

Formal awards and decorations within the Israeli Army carry significant prestige because so few are given; therefore, those that are given are recognized as being especially deserving. There are three basic Israeli decorations: one for good conduct, one for bravery, and one for heroism. From 1948 through the 1973 war, approximately 1,000 good conduct medals, 100 medals (Etour Haoz) for bravery, and fewer than 20 medals (Etour Hgevora) for heroism were awarded.[53] This is extraordinary by standards of most other armies, considering that the IDF was engaged in four major wars and numerous smaller conflicts during this period. The annual award by the President of Israel of a certificate of honor to 100 outstanding conscripts and career soldiers is also much sought after by the Israeli soldier as a mark of special recognition and esteem.

Little utilized but available to the Israeli officer is a military justice system that authorizes court-martial and administrative application of the law. Possible punishments include restriction to the unit area, loss of pay, reprimand, loss of rank, life imprisonment, and the death penalty. The last two penalties have never been used against an IDF member.[54] When used as punishment, the military justice system has been used primarily against conscripts with criminal records who attempt to continue their life of crime within the IDF. Some use has also been made against those few soldiers who go against the group norms and indulge in drugs (primarily hashish).

Legitimate Power

The weakest source of the Israeli leader's power to influence his soldiers is probably legitimate power. As the only source of power that is impersonal and primarily dependent upon insignia of rank and position, it has less influence over the behavior of Israeli soldiers than do the other sources of power. The lack of significant authority figures in Israeli culture and the questioning nature of the Israeli soldier make the exercise of power merely on the basis of rank or position a doubtful one. For this reason, rank is worn casually in the Israeli Army and primarily identifies the leader to be followed rather than one to be obeyed:

> It may be said that the concept of discipline in the Israeli Army is limited to the need for unquestionable obedience in executing orders, while dispensing with the symbols of submission. These may be necessary ingredients [in some armies], but they are vital only when there is a great discrepancy

between ranks as regards motivation, orientation, and cour-age.[55]

The fact that the IDF has been the main instrument ensuring the survival of the State of Israel since 1948 has earned the Israeli Defense Forces enormous legitimacy in the eyes of all Israelis, including its own soldiers. In this sense, great legitimacy is granted to IDF leaders but not on the basis of rank alone. Rolbant points to the ineffectiveness of an attempt to increase "formal respect for superiors":

> He issued orders for soldiers to say "Yes, Commander." The soldiers did so. Nothing happened, except that the soldiers now said "Yes, Commander," as ordered. The change was of no educational value and was scrapped . . . obviously external symbols cannot be automatically imposed since they belong to the climate in which they grow; and Israeli society is still possessed of few non-utilitarian graces such as adorn a more stable society which is neither hard-pressed nor in a hurry to assert itself. . . .[56]

Expert Power

Israeli officers and NCOs are the product of a unique selection and training process that make them the best qualified leaders in the Middle East to deal with the terrain and type of battle likely to be faced by the Israeli Defense Forces in any future wars. Because their anticipated area of operations is so limited and because the experience gained in four major conflicts since 1948 is so plentiful, the Israelis have the luxury of focusing their preparations for defense upon a relatively narrow range of problems. Interior lines of communications, training on future battlegrounds, and the unique type of combined-arms desert warfare perfected by the IDF have presented the Israeli with a well-defined arena and allowed the IDF to produce leaders for that arena that are unmatched by any other army.

Israeli soldiers have come to expect that their leaders are the most expert and most capable leaders possible. Almost all Israeli males are drafted. From the complete cross section of Israeli society, conscripts with the most leadership potential are selected early to attend NCO and officer schools. There is no central military academy. All potential officers attend a basic course and then are sent to specialized schools (for example, infantry or armor).

Two characteristics appear to be common to all instruction, however. First, care is taken to ensure that all conscripts, officer candidates, and ordinary soldiers train in every area of the country so that they all become very familiar with its geography. Second, IDF leaders, both officers and NCOs, are repeatedly taught "that the contagion of courage is the source of all battlefield unity and unity secures success in the field." [57]

There is little doubt in the Israeli soldier's mind that his leaders are the most expert in the Middle East; they have proven that point repeatedly over the past 30 or more years. This perceived expertise and the confidence it imparts to the collective unit in facing combat provide a source of tremendous influence for the small-unit leader in the Israeli Army.

Referent Power

Without doubt, the intense identification of most Israeli soldiers with their leaders and, through them, with the nation of Israel and its cause of survival is the most potent source of leader influence within the Israeli Army. The very strong control of the group over the Israeli soldier gives the leader his influence. Interviews of Israeli war veterans illustrate the power of the group, indicating that their behavior was dominated by

> the need to fulfill their obligation toward their fellow soldier, "the affilitative motive" as it has been called . . . [and] fear of shame, of possible ostracism or disapproval they might experience . . . everybody knew where you were . . . what you did or failed to do.[58]

Underlying the strong control of the group over the individual soldier's behavior is an almost universal sense of brotherhood, which exists among officers and enlisted soldiers alike. An unofficial but widely known and repeated address, "The Fellowship of Fighters," by Yitzhak Sadeh illustrates what the Israelis call their tradition of "unconditional" comradeship within the IDF. Although it strikes some as "somewhat naive" or a "trifle corny," it appears to represent the beliefs and attitudes of Israeli soldiers.[59]

> The fellowship of men fighting for a common cause is surely the perfection of comradeship. Without it nothing can be achieved. . . . Who is your comrade? He is the man standing at your side ready to shield your body with his. . . .

> Comradeship has to be nourished. It has to be learned. As you learn to feel that each and every day of the year is the crucial day, so you must learn to know that the friend at your side is your brother in the deepest sense—your comrade in dedication . . . and in act.[60]

Leadership of such soldiers falls to "the man who knows the most . . . is able to motivate his men to make the supreme effort required in battle. The men believe in him, rely on him, and expect him to give them the right orders." [61]

The power of the group is so strong in the Israeli Army that significant breakthroughs have been made using the attraction of the group to treat soldiers suffering from severe psychological trauma or battle shock. Israeli standard procedure has been to evacuate "battle stress" casualties much as other casualties were evacuated. Few if any of these casualties ever returned to their units, and the traumatic effects often lasted for years. Beginning in the early 1970s, however, the Israeli Army, because of significant numbers of such casualties, assigned "battlefield psychologists" to units and began a program of treating such casualties at the front; "in most cases, they could hear or even see the battle." The power and attraction of the group were used to assist in the "psychiatric first aid," which was administered in the context of the patient's daily regimen within his unit. Results of this new treatment have been very encouraging. Over 80 percent of such casualties, previously lost to the unit, are now reintegrated with their units as fully functioning soldiers.[62]

The significance of such cohesive units and the enormous influence Israeli leaders have within their units are often not realized by outsiders. One illustration of the significance of cohesion is the role it has played in Israeli victories over Arab armies that significantly lack cohesion and the leadership necessary to create it.[63]

TABLE 10

Characteristics of Leadership

Element	North Vietnamese	United States	Soviet	Israeli
	Army			
Leadership priority focused on small units, platoon, and company	+ +	–	–	+ +
Strict code of professional ethics requires leaders to share danger and hardship	+ +	+ +	+	+ +
Leaders utilize effects of civic education or indoctrination to maximize leadership	+ +	–	+	+
Small-unit leaders have authority to control all events or actions in unit	+ +	–	+	+
Leader influence through power to reward and punish	+ +	–	+	+
Leader influence through expertise and as source of information	+ +	+	+	+
Leader influence through legitimate power	+ +	+	+	+ +
Leader influence through referent power	+ +	+	+	+ +

Legend: Strong + +
+
–
Weak --

CHAPTER IX

Conclusions

M AJOR DIFFERENCES in cohesion and in the factors that promote it exist among the four armies studied. The North Vietnamese and the Israeli armies have achieved significant degrees of cohesion and combat effectiveness through policies designed to promote cohesion and to take advantage of positive and negative societal effects on their armed forces. A product of a very unique society and political system, the Soviet Army has relied primarily on its ability to control its soldiers totally, to manage manifestations of societal conflict within the Soviet Army, and to use the great legitimacy of the "motherland" within Soviet society to create some cohesive and effective units—but units still with major defects. Only in the US Army have policies and practices been instituted that consistently fail to promote cohesion.

The US Army faces fundamental cohesion and effectiveness problems. Largely as a result of a mode of decisionmaking based on emphasizing the quantifiable and easily measured factors involved in cost-effectiveness analysis and also as a result of political expediency, the US Army, over the past two decades, has arrived at a set of policies that permeate almost all aspects of the organization—personnel, legal, logistical, and operational—

and prevent the implementation of practices necessary to create cohesive units.

Recent attempts to institute a regimental system indicate recognition of the problem. Unfortunately, even if successfully implemented as now planned, the regimental system will not resolve the core problems involved in building cohesion at squad, platoon, and company levels.

The NVA and Israeli armies are almost textbook examples of how to create and maintain a cohesive army within the context of each army's unique society and political system. Both recognize that modern warfare requires that the successful army rely upon a strong sense of internalized discipline that places loyalty and responsibility to unit objectives as the highest good. NVA and Israeli leaders recognized the need for an internalized control system, and each in its geographic area of conflict created an army surpassing any other in the "human element." Positive control down to the individual soldier was ensured within each army by binding him to his unit through creating unit stability and integrity and by ensuring that the unit provided the basis for the soldier's primary social affiliation. Within each army, the primary group or small unit formed the "cutting edge" of the organization—the instrument that could physically achieve the policy objectives sought by each army. This "cutting edge" was maintained through a normative control system that emphasized service and responsibility to the unit or group. Commonality of values through socialization or resocialization once in the army, peer surveillance, demands for conformity, and the individual soldier's personal conviction that he was fully committed to his term of service all worked to maintain the pervasive influence of the small group over the behavior of the individual soldier for the purpose of achieving objectives in both armies.

Societal impacts on both armies were not significant hindrances to the promotion of cohesion, and in most cases the potential for nationalism contributed significantly to the commonality of values and ability to communicate necessary to create cohesive units. North Vietnamese and Israeli soldiers were also exposed to an intense resocialization process that, building upon common cultural values, established dominant rules of behavior under the control of small-unit leaders. A significant difference between the two armies occurred in policies designed to maintain the dominance of the small unit over the behavior of the individual soldiers. Within the North Vietnamese Army fighting in South Vietnam, isolation was effectively used to separate main force soldiers from extended or significant contact with civilians or non-unit members. Within the Israeli Army, frequent contact with other unit members was the general practice, but only because of demanding training and operational requirements that tended to keep soldiers close to their units. When extended contacts with Israeli civilians occurred, the cohesive norms of the small unit were generally reinforced by a supportive Israeli population—a factor that did not generally exist for the NVA within South Vietnam.

Leadership and accompanying policies evident in the approach to leadership in the Israeli and North Vietnamese armies are excellent; they significantly promote cohesion. In both armies, leadership at the small-unit level is given priority. The best leaders available in each society are dedicated to their respective armies and to the task of controlling the many small groups that emerge in all armies; they lead these groups to achieve the objectives of each army. In both armies, leadership authority is maximized to promote the leader's ability to influence and control his unit. Authority in these armies is not centralized at higher levels; small-unit leaders have the necessary authority to build cohesive units and have generally succeeded in using positive societal effects to promote cohesion, while blocking or minimizing negative societal effects.

Through careful management of soldier assignments and other policies at the unit level, the Soviet Army has been able to control the negative effects of ethnic conflict and of other sources of conflict evident within Soviet society. Within the high-priority, mostly Slavic units of the Soviet Army, relatively little ethnic conflict exists. On the other hand, such conflict does exist in construction and other low-priority units that receive a greater mix of ethnic types. For some purposes, it appears that the Soviets have created two different armies. In one, they seem willing to accept ethnic conflict and loss of cohesion in order to avoid the dangers of creating "national" units and to promote "Russification" of Soviet society. In the second—the more elite combat units, comprised of more "reliable" Slavs—the Soviets appear to have achieved a remarkable degree of cohesion.

Underlying the cohesion the Soviets have achieved in their priority units are two major factors. Through unit-level policies, the Soviet Army ensures that the Soviet soldier's main social affiliations and his dominant primary group are almost always found within the soldier's immediate unit. The other factor is the enormous degree of legitimacy within Soviet society attributed to the state or the "motherland" and to the Army as the principal defender of these almost universal values.

Although strong primary groups exist within Soviet units and although they usually give full patriotic support to the motherland and accept the legitmacy of the Soviet Army, they do not always develop small-group norms congruent with Soviet Army objectives. Upper-level Soviet leaders recognize the requirement for a normative approach to leadership, based more upon personal relationships between small-unit leaders and their soldiers, and to some extent are taking measures to further it. Little progress has been achieved in these efforts because of serious systemic defects that are well entrenched in the policies and practices that dominate the current Soviet approach; these are manifested in how the Soviet Army selects, trains, and controls NCOs and junior officers. Though also true of the overall Soviet approach, the system that guides lower-level unit leaders rewards narrow specialization with limited responsibility and a rigid, managerial, nonpersonal approach in dealing with subordinates. Nowhere below the general staff level does there appear to be an institutional focus where responsibility rests. Instead, especially at lower-level units, commanders appear to spend significant time and effort ensuring that they are not responsible. Soviet Army leaders are further hindered in promoting cohesion by severe limitations on the initiative they are allowed, especially at the small-unit level. They are expected to follow regulations and operational plans exactly. Though the need for initiative is recognized, especially if the normative approach necessary to cohesion is to be implemented, the system actually tolerates little initiative. Because of the system's need to fix responsibility for any failure, the exercise of initiative usually exposes the leader to criticism or more severe action. As a result, leaders are careful to abide fully by the rules and written guidance. If there is then a failure, they cannot be held responsible.

Given the nature of the Soviet system, the development of a normative leadership approach necessary to promote military cohesion characterized by congruence between small-group norms and Army objectives is unlikely. As a result, the cohesion that presently exists within small units will probably support the established Soviet style of warfare where small units and their leaders are expected to meet objectives according to an established and well-regulated plan. Given unexpected contingencies and the "friction" of war, especially at the small-unit level, cohesion within Soviet units will tend to unravel as small units and their leaders become increasingly unable to cope with rapidly developing and unexpected situations.

Alone among the four armies studied, the US Army has lost control over the individual soldier to the extent that the creation of cohesive units is extremely difficult in all except some elite ranger and airborne or geographically-isolated units. For most US soldiers, the unit does not provide the source of primary social affiliations. As a result, the American soldier tends to seek esteem, recognition, and his main social affiliations beyond the influence of his unit and his leaders. The inability of the US Army to maintain small-unit integrity and stability strongly reinforces the transient nature of the small unit. Not only the individual replacement system but the failure to bind the soldier to his unit through traditional means and through positive unit control over the good things in a soldier's life hinders cohesion and contributes to the soldier's being controlled by actions and people beyond his unit.

Underlying this basic failure is a primary assumption of the volunteer Army: You can pay a person enough to be a good soldier. To assume that the soldier is primarily an economic man and can be motivated primarily through utilitarian means denies the US Army the strongest motivation possible on the battlefield—the small unit with its leader, held together by a common calling and strong and mutual expectations about the behavior of each other on the battlefield.

Outside the US Army, broad societal factors militate against the building of cohesive units. Disagreement over the past two decades among American political, economic, and other elites about the proper US international role and about foreign policy goals has contributed significantly to the erosion of a supportive military ethos within the civilian elite.[1] This has been reflected in numerous ways that affect the Army's ability to create and maintain cohesive units. The end of the draft and the ease with which a soldier can presently escape the inconvenience and hardship of Army life and return to civilian life with little penalty hinder the promotion of cohesion.

The shift to an occupational model, rather than a vocational one, has tended to weaken the ideological national values that traditionally contributed to cohesion. Today's US soldiers tend to be recruited from those segments of the American populace with the least developed sense of civic consciousness and national values. These recruits are vaguely aware of the Presidency but have little other political knowledge. However, this appears to matter little, if at all, to defense policymakers, as long as quantitative recruiting objectives are met.[2]

The combined effects of recruitment policies, internal Army policies, and societal effects deny small-unit leaders the opportunity to build cohesive units. High recruit pay, permanent pass policies, liberal release policies, turbulence, social affiliation with outside groups, living off post, cost-effective barracks and messes, and many other factors identified earlier in this study all work to ensure that the small US unit remains a fragmented group unable to coalesce around its leaders to produce a cohesive unit.

Recommendations

Current organization and practices within the Army deny the US soldier the degree of social support from his fellow soldiers provided in other armies and necessary to build cohesive units able to compete as equals with those of possible enemies.

Sound principles observed in almost all other major armies for maximizing the human potential of soldiers have been sacrificed in the name of expediency to accommodate the perceived dictates of the American political and domestic environments. The American people must be asked to sacrifice if we are to field a capable, dependable Army. Current pronouncements as to the good health of the Army are being made about an organization that has only successfully adapted to the imperatives of American domestic politics, not one that has been tested by the stress of war.

To create a cohesive Army with the desirable characteristics described in earlier chapters, significant changes must take place. Specifically, I recommend the following:

1. The US Armed Forces must return to the service motivation of earlier years that held that all Americans owe some contribution to the well-being of their country. As part of this approach, pay scales for all first-termers, enlisted and officers, should be reduced. Sergeants and officers should be representative of the best available in American society. Overall, the Army should be comprised of citizen soldiers representative of all strata of American society. This should be accompanied by a reemphasis on patriotism and a resocialization of American values that holds as a first principle that each American is responsible in some significant way for the continuation of a strong American democracy.

2. The US Army must assign soldiers and leaders to company and lower-level units permanently. The spare-parts mentality produced by the MOS system, one that allows soldiers of like MOS to be readily interchangeable, must no longer be the primary working principle of the Army's personnel management system. Company and lower-level units should be the objects of personnel management, not individual soldiers. In this regard, the regimental system misses the mark and should be deemphasized in favor of current test programs focusing on personnel stability in company and lower-level units.

3. The US Army must move away from the utilitarian or econometric system presently used to attract and motivate soldiers. Instead, the US soldier must draw his primary motivation from within his unit and from his immediate leaders. Mess halls, barracks, and other facilities as well as numerous other practices and personnel policies must be decentralized and restructured to turn the soldier toward his unit as the primary source for satisfying his social and security needs in his day-to-day life.

4. The US Army must initiate internal reforms to allow leaders, especially company-level officers, the authority to regain leadership control over the US soldier, his time, and his associations in order to permit the small-unit leader the opportunity to become the dominant influence in the day-to-day life of the US soldier.

A comprehensive set of recommendations that would fill out the main points outlined above would include most of the criteria for cohesion I have discussed throughout. The Army must turn from its drift into a utilitarian or econometric system for controlling and motivating soldiers. Over the past two decades, small-unit leaders have lost their ability to build and maintain unit cohesion as the Army adapted to cost-effectiveness measures and an unsympathetic domestic environment during the Vietnam years. The Congress, the courts, the executive branch, and even the Army initiated changes during the late 1960s and early 1970s in efforts to ease the Army's passage among increasingly hostile elements of American society. Accompanying these major changes was a significant shift in authority away from junior leaders at the squad, platoon, and company levels. To save money, attract recruits, and preclude "embarrassing incidents," authority was increasingly centralized at higher levels. This shift was reinforced by senior staffs who, sensing the trend, became very risk conscious and attempted to protect commanders with "safe-sided" advice, with resource managers, with judge advocate generals, and with public affairs officers especially, who gave counsel with little or no thought to effect on unit cohesion. Although this action protected the commander, it also made the task that he and lower-level leaders had of building cohesive, combat-ready units much more difficult. There are, of course, some drawbacks to decentralization. Local abuses resulting from increased authority can and will occur, but these are far outweighed by the benefits of decentralization.

The net effect of many of the changes over the years has been to make the junior leaders, especially the NCO, more of a bystander, as higher ranking officers reduced the junior leader's authority and curtailed much of his traditional responsibility. A recent Forces Command (FORSCOM) commander, General Shoemaker, recognized this problem, noting that "NCOs are not fully utilized while commanders and other senior officers are working as hard as they can.''

Accompanying this significant loss of authority and diminution of function over the past two decades have been other changes within the NCO corps. The soldier population within the All-Volunteer Army from which most NCOs are recruited is significantly less well-qualified than it was in previous years. A basic requisite for cohesion is that immediate leaders be recognized and respected as representative of the best a society has to offer. Those soldiers who are more representative of American society, however, tend not to reenlist and are lost as potential NCOs, leaving primarily "unrepresentative" soldiers as the main source of enlisted leaders. In fiscal year 1982, a good reenlistment year, approximately 47 percent of the US Army's reenlistments were in category IV, the category having the least qualified personnel.

> The US Army must move to increase the quality of small-unit leadership by ensuring that NCOs are representative of American society and that NCO authority is restored to the degree necessary for building cohesive units. Many actions would promote this goal, but one of the most important is the restoration at squad and platoon levels of the NCO's authority to control his soldiers 24 hours a day. As a first step, such action means restoration of the pass as a privilege under NCO control.
>
> The degree to which an army should be isolated from the society that supports it has long been a question among military sociologists. There doesn't appear to be a definitive answer, even for a particular army. One answer depends upon the degree to which surrounding societal values support the small-unit norms necessary for cohesion. Within the Israeli, North Vietnamese, and Soviet armies, soldiers are isolated to the degree necessary for the leader and group to become the dominant influence in the soldier's daily life. The Soviet Army requires significantly more isolation than the Israeli Army, which receives very strong societal support for its

unit norms. In the North Vietnamese Army, isolation varied. In the North and in areas in the South under firm North Vietnamese control, isolation of soldiers was not extensive. In South Vietnam, where much of the population was reluctant to support either side, North Vietnamese Army isolation was much more pronounced. Presently, the US Army needs to institutionalize a greater degree of isolation in order to allow small-unit leaders to regain control of their units and build cohesion. Such isolation need not be extensive and probably would not exceed the isolation necessary in the 1950s and the early 1960s, when low pay, NCO authority, and other factors tended to orient the US soldier toward his unit 24 hours a day.

A related recommendation is to regain from the courts and the Judge Advocate General authority for NCOs to maintain discipline in their own right. They should not have to clear their actions with higher commanders through an unwieldy and unresponsive military justice system that has decreased the leader's authority by placing priority on individual rights over unit discipline and cohesion. It is time to return to the principle of past years; it is in accordance with democratic tradition that soldiers give up some of their individual rights while they serve. At the same time, it must also be recognized that the principles of war are autonomous—they operate independently of political or social system. Neither democracy nor any other form of government is assured an army more capable than another's. This is especially true when citizens in a democracy forget that personal sacrifices are necessary to build an army and when they become increasingly self-indulgent—lacking the self-discipline necessary to fulfill their responsibilities, while missing few opportunities to assert their rights.

APPENDIX

On Why Soldiers Fight*

Many investigations of why men fight have focused on the concepts of morale or esprit de corps and have discussed individual and unit performance in combat in terms of courage, discipline, enthusiasm, and willingness to endure hardship. Such research, however, does not adequately explain the factors involved in the endurance of a modern professional army.

According to Morris Janowitz (1964), "even in the smallest unit there is an 'iron framework' of organization which serves as a basis of social control. The single concept of military morale must give way, therefore, to a theory of organizational behavior in which an array of sociological concepts is employed" (Janowitz and Little, 1965; George, 1967; Moskos, 1980; Kellet, 1982).

The literature on military motivation suggests a number of explanations for human behavior in combat. These approaches treat the primary group and its relationship to the organization in explaining combat behavior. Beginning with Shils and Janowitz in their study of cohesion and disintegration in the Wehrmacht,

---

*Portions of this appendix were previously printed in Wm. Darryl Henderson's *Why the Vietcong Fought*, and are reprinted here with permission of the Greenwood Press, Westport, Conn.

small-group cohesion, interaction within the group, and organization have been increasingly emphasized.

By the term *primary group*, investigators refer to the concept of *Gemeinschaft* (small, intimate, community relationships). More specifically, primary groups have been conceptualized as being

> characterized by intimate face-to-face association and co-operation. They are primary in several senses, but chiefly in that they are fundamental in forming the social nature and ideals of the individual. The result of intimate association . . . is a certain fusion of individualities into a common whole, so that one's very self, for many purposes at least, is the common life and purpose of the group. Perhaps the simplest way of describing this wholeness is by saying it is a "we." [1]

Research indicates that the soldier is strongly bound to the primary group as long as it is capable of satisfying his major physiological and social needs. Shils and Janowitz reported that as long as the Wehrmacht soldier had the necessary resources and as long as the primary group met his essential personal needs, he was "bound by the expectations and demands of its other members." Molnar (1965) cites similar evidence discussing soldiers bound to some degree by social role and status patterns common to a primary group. Shils and Janowitz state:

> It appears that a soldier's ability to resist is a function of the capacity of his immediate primary group [his squad or section] to avoid social disintegration. When the individual's immediate group, and its supporting formations, met his basic organic needs, offered him affection and esteem from both officers and comrades, supplied him with a sense of power and adequately regulated his relations with authority, the element of self-concern in battle, which would lead to disruption of the effective functioning of his primary group was minimized. [2]

Supporting this basic hypothesis, Shils and Janowitz also note:

> For the ordinary German soldier the decisive fact was that he was a member of a squad or section which maintained its structural integrity and which coincided roughly with the social unit which satisfied some of his major primary needs. He was likely to go on fighting, provided he had the necessary

weapons, as long as the group possessed leadership with which he could identify himself, and as long as he gave affection to and received affection from the other members of his squad and platoon. In other words, as long as he felt himself to be a member of his primary group and therefore bound by the expectations and demands of its other members, his soldierly achievement was likely to be good.[3]

Additional factors also impact upon the cohesiveness of the primary group and its influence on the behavior of the soldier. Many investigators have pointed out that the concept of the primary group takes on an added sharpness under combat conditions. In considering the primary group as a dependent variable, the mere fact that a combat situation entails an increase in solidarity in response to an external threat is a phenomenon that has been verified many times. When a threat and the responsibilities for coping with it are shared, an increase in group solidarity and a reduction of internal group conflict usually occur. Observers of men in combat have called attention "again and again to the fact that the most significant persons for the combat soldier are the men who fight by his side and share with him the ordeal of trying to survive."[4] S. L. A. Marshall, an observer of men in combat in numerous wars, observes: "I hold it to be one of the simplest truths of war that the thing which enables an infantry soldier to keep going with his weapon is the near presence or the presumed presence of a comrade."[5]

Another variable that seems to increase primary group cohesion in combat is the soldier's calculation of his chances for escape from the threatening situation. If he is bound to the primary group by isolation from surrounding groups, by anxiety-producing doubts about his ability to leave his unit successfully, and by other such ambiguities, he sees his best chance of survival as resting with one or two buddies or with the other members of his primary group (Little, 1964).

Other factors influencing primary group cohesiveness are the past social experiences of the members. Common religion, race, ethnic group, social class, age, geographical region, and history appear to contribute to the communications necessary for intimate interpersonal relationships common to a primary group (Janowitz and Little, 1965; Shils and Janowitz, 1948; Emerson, 1967; Kohn, 1932; George, 1967).

Another influence shaping primary group solidarity is the member's commitment to his sociopolitical system, ideology, secondary group symbols, and causes, such as common awareness and resentment of the nation's colonial history (George, 1976). In this concept of "latent ideology," Moskos attributes some importance to broad sociopolitical values in explaining why men fight (Moskos, 1975). Indoctrination induces commitment to secondary symbols by establishing preconditions for primary group cohesion. Indoctrination themes generally stress the legitimacy of war aims and justify fighting for such aims (George, 1967). While recognizing the impact of secondary groups on the individual soldier, Shils and Janowitz maintain that their infuence is slight, compared to that of the primary group. They quote a German soldier in support of their position:

> The company [military unit] is the only truly existent community. This community allows neither time nor rest for a personal life. It forces us into its circle, for life is at stake. Obviously compromises must be made and claims be surrendered. . . . Therefore the idea of fighting, living, and dying for the fatherland, for the cultural possessions of the fatherland, is but a relatively distant thought. At least it does not play a great role in the practical motivations of the individual.[6]

The honor and romanticism involved in fighting a war often appeal to the young soldier who experiences the need for asserting manliness or toughness. The coincidence of these personal needs with similar group norms and military codes also serves to reinforce group solidarity (Shils and Janowitz, 1948; Stouffer et al., 1949; Moskos, 1970).

This discussion has emphasized the influence of the primary group in shaping the behavior of the soldier. However, a significant question remains. Will the primary group produce behavior by the soldier that is congruent with the goals of the organization? Many investigators have noted that the primary group cohesiveness that emerges in the small combat unit can militate either for or against the goals of the formal military organization (Etzioni, 1961; Janowitz and Little, 1965; George, 1967). For example, in discussing problems of "Negro" US Army units during World War II, Janowitz and Little point out:

Primary groups can be highly cohesive and yet impede the goals of military organizations. Cohesive primary groups contribute to organizational effectiveness only when the standards of behavior they enforce are articulated with the requirements of formal authority.[7]

Still other investigators have found small group behavior in combat situations that is deviant from the organization's point of view (Shils and Janowitz, 1948; George, 1967; Little, 1964). Shils and Janowitz in their investigation of cohesion and disintegration in the Wehrmacht found that units that surrendered as a group were led by "soft-core," non-Nazi comrades to whom organizational goals were relatively unimportant.[8]

The performance of the group in meeting organizational goals is largely dependent upon the effectiveness of the leader. Research suggests that a capable leader can manipulate primary group members through a wide range of organizational mechanisms, psychological techniques, and indoctrination themes in order to shape primary group norms and attitudes that are compatible with organizational objectives. He can accomplish this task because he has been accepted as the natural leader of the small group. Men who fight modern wars must be convinced that their leaders have their welfare in mind, and leaders must continually demonstrate expertise and set the example in adhering to group norms before men will follow them (Dollard, 1943; Homans, 1946; Marshall, 1947; Shils and Janowitz, 1948; Stouffer, 1949; Little, 1964; George, 1967; Van Creveld, 1982).

Primary group behavior, whether deviant or desirable from the organization's point of view, is the result of norms formed by primary group interaction. The primary group is therefore a major factor in explaining man's behavior (positive or negative) in combat.

A recent and convincing study comparing the "fighting power" or human capabilities of the World War II German and US armies reinforces the major conclusions in the above review of the literature on why soldiers fight. In the study, Martin Van Creveld notes:

. . . [The soldier] fought for the reasons that men have always fought: because he felt himself a member of a well-integrated, well-led team whose structure, administration, and functioning were perceived to be . . . equitable and just.[9]

In studying the Israeli Defense Forces in all of their wars, including the war in Lebanon, Rueven Gal distinguishes between combat and preparation for combat in discussing why soldiers fight. His research indicates that in actual combat soldiers fight because of the desire to survive and because of the cohesive effects of the small group and its leadership. In preparing for combat, group cohesion and leadership are again very significant along with two other factors: the confidence the individual has in himself as a soldier within the context of his training, weapons, and ability to meet any anticipated situation and the perceived legitimacy of the "war" within the public and unit. However, legitimacy was not requisite. In Lebanon, as long as Israeli troops had confidence in their leaders at the company level and below and as long as cohesion was strong, they continued the advance, even if they disagreed with the immediate objective or questioned the overall legitimacy of the "invasion." [10]

Again the conclusion that cohesion, common values, and leadership must be viewed within an overall approach that considers individual, organizational, situational, and social factors in explaining why men fight is strongly reinforced.

ENDNOTES

CHAPTER I

1. U.S.G. Sharp and W.C. Westmoreland, *Report on the War in Vietnam* (Washington, DC: Government Printing Office, 1968), pp. 107–207.

2. The North Vietnamese Army included "Vietcong" Main Force Units formed from "Regroupees" who returned to the South after the defeat of the French and the failure to hold unifying elections. North Vietnamese control of Vietcong forces was firm in all areas, not only operationally but also including control of internal organization and policies within Vietcong Main Force units. Soldiers from the North were always present in Vietcong units and their numbers increased as the war continued.

3. Van Tien Dung, "On Experiences in Building the Revolutionary Armed Strength of Our Party." Taken from a paper presented at the American Political Science Association Convention in San Francisco, September 1975; "The Political Role and Development of the Peoples' Army of Vietnam," by William S. Turley, Southern Illinois University, Carbondale, Ill., 1975.

4. Wm. Darryl Henderson, *Why the Vietcong Fought: A Study of Motivation and Control in a Modern Army in Combat* (Westport, Conn.: Greenwood Press, 1979), pp. 119–35.

5. Ibid.

6. One of the few analysts to consider the "human element" in assessing the opposing forces in the Falklands war was William T. Taylor, Jr., in an article on the Falklands war, *Christian Science Monitor*, 17 June 1982, p. 1.

7. T.N. Dupuy, *Numbers, Predictions, and War* (New York: Bobbs-Merrill, 1979). An interesting method of predicting war outcomes based on assigning numerical weights to various factors (offensive or defensive posture, logistics,

weather, terrain, communications, firepower, strength, equipment, morale and leadership, and others) determined to be significant factors through historical study. Although morale and leadership are considered to "probably have more influence on the outcome of a battle than any of the other qualitative variables of combat," no method of assessing or comparing these factors is offered other than indicating that the weighting process for these variables is highly suggestive.

8. John H. Johns et al., *Cohesion in the US Military* (Washington, DC: National Defense University Press, 1984), p. 9.

9. Henderson, *Why the Vietcong Fought*, pp. 3–18.

10. Mao Tse-tung, in *The Chinese Communist Army in Action* by Alexander George (New York: Columbia University Press, 1967), p. 25.

11. Martin Van Creveld, *Fighting Power* (Westport, Conn.: Greenwood Press, 1982). In a recent work that again demonstrates the significance of the small group, leadership, and military cohesion in combat, the author compares the internal personnel practices, policies, and leadership of the Wehrmacht and the US Army in World War II and concludes that the Wehrmacht was a far superior army in its human capabilities.

12. Edward A. Shils and Morris Janowitz, "Cohesion and Disintegration in the Wehrmacht in World War II," *Public Opinion Quarterly* 12 (1948): 281.

13. Alexander L. George, "Primary Groups, Organization and Military Performance," *The Study of Leadership* (West Point: USMA Printing Plant, 1972), p. 19–3.

14. S.L.A. Marshall, *Men Against Fire* (New York: William Morrow, 1947), p. 42.

15. Johns, *Cohesion in the US Military*, pp. 61–62.

16. Erich M. Remarque, *All Quiet on the Western Front* (New York: Fawcett-Crest, 1975), p. 186.

17. James Webb, *Fields of Fire* (Englewood Cliffs: Prentice-Hall, 1978), p. 258.

18. Anthony Kellett, *Combat Motivation: The Behavior of Soldiers in Battle* (Boston: Kluwer, 1982), p. 97.

19. Morris Janowitz and Roger Little, *Sociology and the Military Establishment* (New York: Russell Sage Foundation, 1965).

20. Kellet, *Combat Motivation*, p. 333.

21. Henderson, *Why the Vietcong Fought*.

22. For a more detailed discussion of the concepts and sources outlined in chapter 3, see a review of the literature in the appendix.

23. For example, see Kellet, *Combat Motivation*. This work is based on a study of US, British, and Canadian Armed Forces.

CHAPTER II

1. John H. Johns et. al., *Cohesion in the US Military* (Washington, DC: National Defense University Press, 1984), p. 9.

2. Karl von Clausewitz, *On War*, trans. Michael Howard and Peter Paret (Princeton: Princeton University Press, 1976), p. 87.

3. Richard T. LaPiere, *A Theory of Social Control* (New York: McGraw-Hill, 1954), pp. 130–188.

4. Amitai Etzioni, *A Comparative Analysis of Complex Organizations* (New York: Free Press, 1975), p. 61.

CHAPTER IV

1. Wm. Darryl Henderson, *Why the Vietcong Fought: A Study of Motivation and Control in a Modern Army in Combat* (Westport, Conn.: Greenwood Press, 1979), pp. 107–118.

2. US Embassy, Saigon, Document No. 1, *Vietnam Documents and Research Notes*, "Diary of an Infiltrator," 1967, pp. 3–5.

3. Henderson, *Why the Vietcong Fought*, p. 117.

4. US Embassy, Saigon, Document No. 102, *Vietnam Documents and Research Notes*, "Diary of an Infiltrator," 1967, pp. 43–44.

5. *Vietnam Interviews*, Interview "K–5" (Santa Monica, Calif.: Rand Corporation, K Series), pp. 32–33.

6. *Interviews*, "K–5," pp. 8–9 and "K–22," pp. 7–8.

7. Charles C. Moskos, "The Sociology of the All-Volunteer Force," a paper presented at the annual meeting of the American Sociological Association, Toronto, Canada, 24–28 August 1981, p. 13.

8. This observation is based upon personal experience as a battalion commander and upon similar observations by other battalion and company commanders.

9. Moskos, "The Sociology of the All-Volunteer Force," pp. 5–6.

10. Ibid., p. 13.

11. Herbert Goldhamer, *The Soviet Soldier* (New York: Crane, Russak and Co., 1975), pp. 26–27.

12. Viktor Suvorov, *Inside the Soviet Army* (New York: Macmillan, 1982), p. 175.

13. Jeffrey Record, *Sizing Up the Soviet Army* (Washington, DC: Brookings Institution, 1975), p. 17.

14. John Erickson and E.J. Feuchtwanger, eds., *Soviet Military Power and Performance* (Hamden, Conn.: Shoe String Press, 1979), pp. 110–11.

15. Andrew J. Rochells and Paul G. Patton, "Demographic Changes in the

USSR: Implications for the Soviet Military" (Washington, DC: Student paper, The National Defense Uniiversity, 1982), pp. 35–36.

16. Ibid., p. 33.

17. Ibid.

18. Drew Middleton, "Racial Clashes Said to Hinder Soviet Forces," *New York Times*, 11 July 1982, p. 9. Andrew Cockburn, *The Threat Inside the Soviet Military Machine* (New York: Random House, 1953). This recent analysis of Soviet military strength appears to have as its primary purpose the discounting of the Soviet military threat to the United States and its allies. Instead of looking at Soviet military capabilities, it emphasizes the many problems and failures of the Soviet military establishment. In the area of the human element or the motivation of Soviet soldiers, the author offers little that is new. Relying on recent studies by Richard Gabriel and the Rand Corporation that used primarily political emigres and ex-soldiers from low priority units as sources, Cockburn presents the Soviet soldier as unreliable, unmotivated, and unthreatening.

19. Stephen Webbe, "A Soviet Soldier's Lot," *Christian Science Monitor*, Midwest Edition, 3 December 1981, pp. B-24–27, B-30.

20. Yitzhak Tarasulo, "The Daily Life of a Soldier in the Modern Soviet Army," Yale University, 1983, presented at the National Convention of the Inter-University Seminar on the Armed Forces and Society, Chicago, October 1983.

21. Erickson and Feuchtwanger, *Soviet Military Power and Performance*, p. 102.

22. S. Enders Wimbush and Alex Alexiev, *The Ethnic Factor in the Soviet Armed Forces* (Santa Monica, Calif.: Rand Corporation, 1982), p. 39.

23. Ibid.

24. The Israeli Defense Force (IDF) is organized around one central staff with one Chief of Staff for the Army, Navy, and Air Force.

25. Samuel Rolbant, *The Israeli Soldier: Profile of an Army* (Cranbury, N.J.: Thomas Yoseloff, 1970), p. 200.

26. Ibid., p. 208.

27. Ibid., p. 200.

28. Ibid., p. 202.

29. *Interviews*, "K-5," p. 24 and "K-4," pp. 7–8.

30. Henderson, *Why the Vietcong Fought*, p. 55.

31. Charles C. Moskos, "From Institution to Occupation: Trends in Military Organization," paper presented at the International Congress, Foundation Society and Armed Forces, The Hague, Netherlands, 9–12 May 1982, pp. 1–3.

32. Moskos, "The Sociology of the All-Volunteer Force," pp. 12–13.

33. Wimbush and Alexiev, *The Ethnic Factor in the Soviet Armed Forces*, p. 13.

34. Goldhamer, *The Soviet Soldier*, pp. 163–64.

35. Wimbush and Alexiev, *The Ethnic Factor in the Soviet Armed Forces*, p. 43.

36. Rolbant, *The Israeli Soldier*, pp. 161–62.

37. Richard F. Nyrop, ed., *Israel: A Country Study* (Washington, DC: American University, 1979), p. 260.

38. Rolbant, *The Israeli Soldier*, p. 215.

39. Henderson, *Why the Vietcong Fought*, pp. 25–47.

40. Ibid.

41. *Interviews*, "K–20," pp. 22–24 and "K–10," p. 16.

42. Ibid., pp. 40–47.

43. *Interviews*, "K–27," p. 18.

44. Wm. Darryl Henderson, "Can-Do NCOs—With Clout—Can Help Cohesion Problem," *Army*, March 1982, p. 20.

45. Ibid., p. 22.

46. Erickson and Feuchtwanger, *Soviet Military Power and Performance*, p. 118.

47. Goldhamer, *The Soviet Soldier*, p. 21.

48. Ibid., pp. 151 and 182.

49. Ibid., p. 192.

50. Ibid., p. 193.

51. Ibid.

52. Wimbush and Alexiev, *The Ethnic Factor in the Soviet Armed Forces*, p. 40.

53. Ibid.

54. Goldhamer, *The Soviet Soldier*, p. 132.

55. Rolbant, *The Israeli Soldier*, p. 107.

56. Ibid., p. 196.

57. Ibid., p. 214.

58. Nyrop, *Israel: A Country Study*, p. 267.

59. US Embassy, Saigon, Document No. 102, pp. 45–47 and *Interviews*, "K–21," p. 7.

60. Moskos, "From Institution to Occupation."

61. Moskos, "The Sociology of the All-Volunteer Force."

62. Henderson, "Can-Do NCOs," p. 21.

63. Moskos, "The Sociology of the All-Volunteer Force," pp. 17–18.

64. Robert L. Goldrich, "Recruiting, Retention, and Quality in the All-Volunteer Force" (Washington, DC: Congressional Research Service, Library of Congress, 1981), pp. 58–59.

65. Ibid., p. 59.

66. V.V. Shelyag, A.D. Glotochkin, and K.K. Platonov, *Military Psychology: A Soviet View* (Moscow, 1972), translated and published by the US Air Force, p. 292.

67. Ibid., p. 176.

68. Ibid., p. 325.

69. Ibid., p. 303.

70. Ibid., p. 344.

71. Goldhamer, *The Soviet Soldier*, p. 184.

72. Erickson and Feuchtwanger, *Soviet Military Power and Performance*, p. 125.

73. Goldhamer, *The Soviet Soldier*, pp. 199–200.

74. Rolbant, *The Israeli Soldier*, p. 160.

75. Ibid., p. 161.

76. Y. Harkabi, "Basic Factors in the Arab Collapse," *Orbis*, Fall 1967.

77. Rolbant, *The Israeli Soldier*, p. 175.

78. Ibid., p. 179.

79. *Interviews*, "K–5," pp. 28–30.

80. Goldrich, "Recruiting, Retention, and Quality in the All-Volunteer Force," pp. 66–65.

81. Shelyag, Glotochkin, and Platonov, *Military Psychology*, p. 320.

82. Ibid., p. 344.

83. Goldhamer, *The Soviet Soldier*, p. 162.

84. Ibid., p. 165.

85. Rolbant, *The Israeli Soldier*, p. 169.

86. Ibid., p. 161.

87. Ibid., p. 198.

88. Ibid., p. 180.

89. Henderson, *Why the Vietcong Fought*, p. 61.

90. Warren L. Young, *Minorities and the Military: A Cross-National Study in World Perspective* (Westport, Conn.: Greenwood Press, 1982), p. 227.

91. Moskos, "The Sociology of the All-Volunteer Force," p. 4.

92. Tom Weber, "Rewarding Things that Count" (Washington, DC: Ft. McNair, Research Directorate, National Defense University, 1982), p. 3-7.

93. Moskos, "The Sociology of the All-Volunteer Force," p. 5.

94. Pete Earley, "Army Urges Rise in Jobs for Women," *Washington Post*, 15 October 1983, p. A3.

95. There is evidence that the Soviets formed an all-Afghan unit comprised of Soviet citizens for deployment in Afghanistan but disbanded it after discipline and control problems arose.

96. Erickson and Feuchtwanger, *Soviet Military Power and Performance*, p. 147.

97. Harriet Fast Scott and William F. Scott, *The Armed Forces of the USSR* (Boulder, Colo.: Westview Press, 1981), p. 389.

98. "More Women Enlist for Soviet Army Duty," *Washington Times*, 28 October 1982, p. 8.

99. Rolbant, *The Israeli Soldier*, p. 208.

100. Irving H. Breslaver, "Women in the Israeli Defense Force," *Retired Officer*, September 1982, pp. 16-19.

101. Nyrop, *Israel: A Country Study*, p. 261.

CHAPTER V

1. E.P. Hollander and R.G. Hunt, eds., *Current Perspectives in Social Psychology* (New York: Oxford Press, 1963), pp. 298-311.

2. John H. Johns et al., *Cohesion in the US Military* (Washington, DC: National Defense University Press, 1984), p. 69.

3. Alexander L. George, "Primary Groups, Organization and Military Performance," in *The Study of Leadership*, Vol. 11 (West Point: USMA Printing Plant, 1973), pp. 20-22—20-23.

4. John Biesanz and Mavis Biesanz, *Modern Society* (Englewood Cliffs: Prentice Hall, 1968), pp. 91-93.

5. This definition of nationalism and the accompanying criteria for measuring its potential are taken largely from a series of lectures delivered by Professor Richard Cottam at the University of Pittsburgh during the summer of 1969. In arriving at this definition Professor Cottam built on the ideas of Hans Kohn and Rupert Emerson. See Hans Kohn, *Nationalism, Its Meaning and History*, rev. ed. (Princeton, N.J.: Van Nostrand, 1965), and Rupert Emerson, *From Empire to Nation* (Boston: Beacon Press, 1967).

6. George, "Primary Groups, Organization and Military Performance," passim.

7. Morris Janowitz, Letter, 22 February 1983.

8. Reuven Gal, "Unit Morale: Some Observations on Its Israeli Version,"

Washington, DC, Department of Military Psychiatry, Division of Neuropsychiatry, Walter Reed Army Institute of Research, 1983, pp. 12-14.

9. Charles C. Moskos, Jr., "The American Combat Soldier in Vietnam," *Journal of Social Issues* 31 (1975): 27.

CHAPTER VI

1. Roy Jumper and Marjorie Weiner Normand, "Vietnam: The Historical Background," in Marvin E. Gentleman, ed., *Vietnam: History, Documents and Opinion* (New York: Fawcett, 1965), pp. 10-28.

2. Ellen Hammer, *Vietnam, Yesterday and Today* (New York: Holt, Rinehart and Winston, 1966), pp. 220-221.

3. Douglas Pike, *Viet Cong, The Organization and Techniques* (Cambridge, Mass.: MIT Press, 1966), p. 374.

4. Hammer, *Vietnam*, p. 39.

5. Pike, *Viet Cong*, p. 2.

6. Ann Crawford, *Customs and Culture of Vietnam* (Tokyo: Tuttle, 1968), pp. 55-61.

7. Henderson, *Why the Vietcong Fought*, p. 53.

8. Hammer, *Vietnam*, p. 1.

9. Martin Patchen, *Black-White Contact in Schools: Its Social and Academic Effects* (West Lafayette, Ind.: Purdue University Press, 1982), p. 349.

10. Morris Janowitz, Letter, 22 February 1983.

11. Charles C. Moskos, "Civic Education and the All-Volunteer Force," paper presented at the IUS symposium on "Civic Education in the Military," 15-16 October 1981, p. 21. See also James N. Rosenau and Ole R. Holsti, "U.S. Leadership in a Shrinking World: The Breakdown of Consensus and the Emergence of Conflicting Belief Systems," *World Politics* 35 (April 1983): 368-92.

12. Hedrick Smith, *The Russians* (New York: Ballantine Books, 1980), p. 405.

13. Ibid., pp. 425-26.

14. Andrew J. Rochells and Paul G. Patton, "Demographic Changes in the U.S.S.R.: Implications for the Soviet Military" (Washington, DC: Student paper, The National Defense University, 1982) p. 29.

15. Ibid.

16. John Erickson and E.J. Feuchtwanger, eds., *Soviet Military Power and Performance* (Hamden, Conn.: Shoe String Press, 1979), p. 146.

17. Smith, *The Russians*, p. 404.

18. Ibid., p. 252.

19. Rochells and Patton, "Demographic Changes in the U.S.S.R.," p. 20.

20. Ibid., p. 24.

21. Robert G. Kaiser, *Russia, The People and the Power* (Brattleboro, Vt.: Book Press, 1976), p. 83.

22. Smith, *The Russians*, p. 83.

23. Herbert E. Meyer, "The Coming Soviet Ethnic Crisis," *Fortune* 98 (4 August 1978): 169.

24. S. Enders Wimbush and Alex Alexiev, *The Ethnic Factor in the Soviet Armed Forces* (Santa Monica, Calif.: Rand Corporation, 1982), p. xiii.

25. Ibid., p. 40.

26. Ibid., p. 40.

27. Rochells and Patton, "Demographic Changes in the U.S.S.R.," pp. 34–35.

28. Ibid., p. 32.

29. Richard F. Nyrop, ed., *Israel: A Country Study* (Washington, DC: American University, 1979), p. 305.

30. Ibid., p. 60.

31. Samuel Rolbant, *The Israeli Soldier: Profile of an Army* (Cranbury, N.J.: Thomas Yoseloff, 1970), p. 228.

32. Nyrop, *Israel*, p. xx.

33. *Vietnam Interviews*, Interview "K-1" (Santa Monica, Calif.: Rand Corporation, 1965–67), p. 28.

34. Michael C. Conley, *The Communist Insurgent Infrastructure in South Vietnam* (Washington, DC: Center for Research in Social Systems, American University, 1966), pp. 302–303.

35. The concept of "latent patriotism" is a useful concept in explaining why soldiers fight. See Charles C. Moskos, "The All-Volunteer Force," in *The Political Education of Soldiers*, Morris Janowitz and Stephen D. Wesbrook, eds. (Beverly Hills, Calif.: Sage Publications, 1983), p. 308.

36. Douglas Pike, *The Vietcong, the Organization and Techniques* (Cambridge, Mass.: MIT Press, 1966), p. 377.

37. Joseph J. Zasloff, *Political Motivation of the Vietcong: The Political Regroupees*, RM–4703/2–ISA/ARPA (Santa Monica, Calif.: Rand Corporation, 1968), p. 40.

38. Alexander George, *The Chinese Communist Army in Action* (New York: Columbia University Press, 1967), p. 89.

39. Moskos, "Civic Education and the All-Volunteer Force," p. 3.

40. Charles C. Moskos, Jr., *The American Enlisted Man* (New York: Russell Sage, 1970), pp. 146–56.

41. Moskos, "Civic Education and the All-Volunteer Force," p. 7.

42. Ibid., p. 11.

43. Ibid., pp. 15–16.

44. Benjamin J. Stein, "The Cheerful Ignorance of the Young in LA," *Washington Post*, 3 October 1983, editorial page.

45. Ibid.

46. Moskos, "Civic Education and the All-Volunteer Force," p. 7.

47. Ibid., p. 19.

48. Ibid., p. 9.

49. Ibid.

50. William E. Odom, "The Militarization of Soviet Society," *Problems of Communism* 25 (September-October 1976): 34–51.

51. Smith, *The Russians*, p. 427.

52. Harriet Fast Scott and William F. Scott, *The Armed Forces of the U.S.S.R.* (Boulder, Colo.: Westview Press, 1981), p. 351.

53. Ibid., p. 380.

54. Odom, "The Militarization of Soviet Society," p. 50.

55. Herbert Goldhamer, *The Soviet Soldier* (New York: Crane, Russak, and Co., 1975), pp. 249–254.

56. Smith, *The Russians*, p. 386.

57. Erickson and Feuchtwanger, *Soviet Military Power and Performance*, p. 103.

58. Smith, *The Russians*, p. 405.

59. Erickson and Feuchtwanger, *Soviet Military Power and Performance*, pp. 101–102.

60. Smith, *The Russians*, p. 332.

61. Ibid., p. 340.

62. Ibid., p. 410.

63. V.V. Shelyag, A.D. Glotochkin, and K.K. Platonov, *Military Psychology: A Soviet View* (Moscow: 1972), translated and published by the US Air Force, pp. 330–55.

64. Goldhamer, *The Soviet Soldier*, pp. 162–163.

65. Rolbant, *The Israeli Soldier*, p. 169.

66. Ibid., p. 206.

67. Ibid., p. 205.

CHAPTER VII

1. Amitai Etzioni, *A Comparative Analysis of Complex Organizations* (New York: Free Press, 1975), p. 61.

2. Anthony Kellet, *Combat Motivation, The Behavior of Soldiers in Battle* (Boston: Kluwer, Nijhoff Publishing, 1982), p. 327.

3. Ibid., p. 330.

4. Ibid.

5. Ibid., p. 332.

6. Wm. Darryl Henderson, *Why the Vietcong Fought: A Study of Motivation and Control in a Modern Army in Combat* (Westport, Conn.: Greenwood Press, 1979), pp. 95–102.

7. Kellet, *Combat Motivation*, p. 327.

8. Henderson, *Why the Vietcong Fought*, pp. 95–102.

9. Wm. Darryl Henderson, "Can-Do NCOs—With Clout—Can Help Cohesion Problems," *Army*, March 1982, pp. 18–22.

10. Henderson, *Why the Vietcong Fought*, p. 72.

11. Ibid., pp. 69–74.

12. John H. Johns et al., *Cohesion in the US Military* (Washington, DC: National Defense University Press, 1984), p. 69.

Henderson, *Why the Vietcong Fought*, p. 73. Much contemporary writing on leadership involves a redefinition of the phenomenon and then a suggested framework for analysis. To move beyond this, analysts must begin to relate and synthesize knowledge from other disciplines. This study attempts to relate a particular view of leadership to a broad body of knowledge about cohesion and its sources among soldiers in several different armies.

Many leadership approaches focus on the sources of the leader's power within the group. The categories of power used here rely primarily upon J.R.P. French, Jr., and B. Raven, "The Bases of Social Power," *The Study of Leadership* (West Point: USMA Printing Plant, 1970), pp. 7-3—7-17.

CHAPTER VIII

1. David W. Elliot and Mai Elliot, *Documents of a VC Delta Unit*, part two (Santa Monica, Calif.: Rand Corporation, 1969), p. 169.

2. *Vietnam Interviews*, Interview "K-14" (Santa Monica, Calif.: Rand Corporation, 1965–67), p. 2.

3. *Interviews*, "K-15," p. 26.

4. Frank Denton, *Volunteers for the Vietcong* (Santa Monica, Calif.: Rand Corporation, 1968), p. vi.

5. *Interviews*, "K-41," p. 14.

6. *Interviews*, "K-9," p. 33.

7. *Interviews*, "K-19," p. 23.

8. *Interviews*, "K-5," pp. 7-15.

9. US Embassy, Saigon, Document No. 72, *Vietnam Documents and Research Notes*, 1967.

10. *Interviews*, "K-5," p. 10.

11. *Interviews*, "K-9," p. 6.

12. *Interviews*, "K-12," p. 9.

13. Ibid.

14. Document No. 22, *Vietnam Documents*, p. 41.

15. *Interviews*, "K-5," pp. 8-9.

16. *Interviews*, "K-12," p. 7.

17. *Interviews*, "K-22," pp. 7-8, 85.

18. *Interviews*, "K-4," pp. 5-6.

19. Charles C. Moskos, "From Institution to Occupation: Trends in Military Organization," paper presented at the International Congress, Foundation Society and Armed Forces, The Hague, Netherlands, 9-12 May 1982, p. 10.

20. While a recent court ruling regarding off-post drug offenses has taken a small step back towards emphasizing unit discipline over individual rights, overall impact on decisions of the past two decades is insignificant.

21. Allen J. Bergstrom, "Ivan is Only About 5'8"," *Air Force*, March 1982, p. 76.

22. V.V. Shelyag, A.D. Glotochkin, and K.K. Platonov, *Military Psychology: A Soviet View* (Moscow: 1972), translated and published by the US Air Force, p. 303.

23. Ibid., p. 324.

24. C. Donnelly, "The Soviet Attitude to Stress in Battle," *Journal of the Royal Army Medical Corps* 128 (1982): 72-73.

25. Ibid., pp. 76-77.

26. Herbert Goldhamer, *The Soviet Soldier: Soviet Military Management at the Troop Level* (New York: Crane Russak & Co., 1975).

27. Harriet F. Scott and William F. Scott, *The Armed Forces of the Soviet Union* (Boulder, Colo: Westview Press, 1981), p. 381.

28. Goldhamer, *The Soviet Soldier*, p. 154.

29. Ibid., p. 156.

30. Ibid.

31. Viktor Suvorov, *Inside the Soviet Army* (New York: Macmillan, 1982), p. 255.

32. Ibid., p. 256.

33. Ibid.

34. V.V. Shelyag et al., *Military Psychology*, p. 328.

35. Ibid., p. 303.

36. Ibid., p. 311.

37. Scott and Scott, *The Armed Forces of the Soviet Union*, p. 380.

38. Goldhamer, *The Soviet Soldier*, p. 178.

39. Scott and Scott, *The Armed Forces of the Soviet Union*, p. 381.

40. Goldhamer, *The Soviet Soldier*, pp. 179–80.

41. Ibid., p. 190.

42. V.V. Shelyag et al., *Military Psychology*, p. 326.

43. Goldhamer, *The Soviet Soldier*, pp. 200–201.

44. V.V. Shelyag et al., *Military Psychology*, p. 303.

45. Suvorov, *Inside the Soviet Army*, p. 236.

46. Ibid., p. 237.

47. Goldhamer, *The Soviet Soldier*, pp. 200–201.

48. Samuel Rolbant, *The Israeli Soldier: Profile of an Army* (New York: Thomas Yoseloff, 1970), p. 175.

49. Ibid.

50. Edward Luttwak and Dan Horowitz, *The Israeli Army* (New York: Harper and Row, 1975), pp. 86–87.

51. Reuven Gal, "Unit Morale: Some Observations on Its Israeli Version," Washington, DC, Department of Military Psychiatry, Division of Neuropsychiatry, Walter Reed Institute of Research, 1983, pp. 8–11.

52. Rolbant, *The Israeli Soldier*, p. 161.

53. Richard F. Nyrop, ed. *Israel, A Country Study* (Washington, DC: The American University, 1978), p. 267.

54. Ibid., p. 269.

55. Rolbant, *The Israeli Soldier*, p. 196.

56. Ibid., p. 197.

57. Ibid.

58. Ibid., p. 161.

59. Yigal Allon, *The Making of Israel's Army* (New York: Universe Books, 1970), p. 131.

60. Ibid., p. 131–132.

61. Rolbant, *The Israeli Soldier*, p. 79.

62. Richard A. Gabriel, "Stress in Battle: Coping on the Spot," *Army*, December 1982, pp. 36–42.

63. Y. Harkabi, "Basic Factors in the Arab Collapse," *Orbis*, Fall 1967.

This is illustrated by a recent observation of officer-soldier relationships in an Arab army. An officer visiting an Arab unit on maneuvers was puzzled by a line of Arab soldiers standing in formation along the side of the officers' briefing and mess tent. The side of the tent was rolled up and the visiting officer could see these soldiers standing there indefinitely. It was not until the direction of the wind shifted and the soldiers were marched around the tent that he realized these soldiers, standing for hours in the sun, were acting as a wind break for the officers' tent.

CHAPTER IX

1. James N. Rosenau and Ole R. Holsti, "US Leadership in a Shrinking World: The Breakdown of Consensus and the Emergence of Conflicting Belief Systems," *World Politics*, vol. 35, no. 3 (April 1983), pp. 368–392.

2. For a more extensive discussion on the shift to an "occupational model" for the Armed Forces, the following readings are recommended: Charles C. Moskos, "From Institution to Occupation: Trends in Military Organization," *Armed Forces and Society*, vol. 4, no. 1. (1977), pp. 41–50 and "Social Considerations of the All-Volunteer Force," in Brent Scowcroft, ed. *Military Service in the United States* (Englewood Cliffs, N.J.: Prentice-Hall, 1982), pp. 129–150.

APPENDIX

1. Charles H. Cooley, *Social Organization* (New York: Charles Scribner's Sons, 1908), introduction.

2. Edward A. Shils and Morris Janowitz, "Cohesion and Disintegration in the Wehrmacht in World War II," *Public Opinion Quarterly* 12 (1948): 281.

3. Ibid., p. 284.

4. Alexander L. George, "Primary Groups, Organizations and Military Performance," *The Study of Leadership* (West Point: USMA Printing Plant, 1972), p. 19-3. For a broader discussion of combat motivation linking primary-group processes to individual self-concern and shared beliefs among soldiers, see Charles Moskos, "Surviving the War in Vietnam," Charles R. Figley and Seymour Leventman, *Strangers at Home: The Vietnam Veteran Since the War* (New York: Praeger, 1980), pp. 71–85.

5. S. L. A. Marshall, *Men Against Fire* (New York: William Morrow, 1947), p. 42.

6. Shils and Janowitz, "Cohesion and Disintegration in the Wehrmacht," p. 284.

7. Morris Janowitz and R. Little, *Sociology and the Military Establishment* (New York: Russel Sage Foundation, 1965), p. 78.

8. Shils and Janowitz, "Cohesion and Disintegration in the Wehrmacht," p. 287.

9. Martin Van Creveld, *Fighting Power: German and US Army Performance, 1939-1945* (Westport, Conn.: Greenwood Press, 1982), pp. 163–164.

10. Reuven Gal, "Unit Morale: Some Observations on Its Israeli Version," Department of Military Psychiatry, Walter Reed Army Institute of Research, Washington, DC, 1983.

BIBLIOGRAPHY

CHAPTERS I-IX

Allon, Yigal. *The Making of Israel's Army*. New York: Universe Books, 1970.

Bergstrom, Allen J. "Ivan is Only About 5 '8 "." *Air Force*, March 1982, p. 76.

Biesanz, John, and Biesanz, Mavis. *Modern Society*. Englewood Cliffs, N.J.: Prentice Hall, 1968.

Breslaver, Irving H. "Women in the Israeli Defense Force." *Retired Officer*, September 1982, pp. 16–19.

Cockburn, Andrew. *The Threat Inside the Soviet Military Machine*. New York: Random House, 1953.

Conley, Michael C. *The Communist Insurgent Infrastructure in South Vietnam*. Washington, DC: Center for Research in Social Systems, American University, 1966.

Crawford, Ann. *Customs and Culture of Vietnam*. Tokyo: Tuttle, 1968.

Denton, Frank. *Volunteers for the Vietcong*. Santa Monica, Calif.: Rand Corporation, 1969.

Donnelly, C. "The Soviet Attitude to Stress in Battle." *Journal of the Royal Army Medical Corps* 128(1982): 72–73.

Dung, Van Tien. "On Experiences in Building the Revolutionary Armed Strength of Our Party." A paper presented at the American Political Science Association Convention in San Francisco, September 1975.

Dupuy, T. N. *Numbers, Predictions, and War*. New York: Bobbs-Merrill, 1979.

Earley, Pete. "Army Urges Rise in Jobs for Women." *Washington Post*, 15 October 1983, p. A3.

Elliot, David W., and Elliott, Mai. *Documents of a VC Delta Unit.* Santa Monica, Calif.,: Rand Corporation, 1969.

Emerson, Rupert. *From Empire to Nation.* Boston: Beacon Press, 1967.

Erickson, John, and Feuchtwanger, E. J., eds. *Soviet Military Power and Performance.* Hamden, Conn.: Shoe String Press, 1979.

Etzioni, Amitai. *A Comparative Analysis of Complex Organizations.* New York: Free Press, 1975.

French, J.R.P., Jr., and Raven, B. "The Bases of Social Power." In *The Study of Leadership.* West Point: USMA Printing Plant, 1970.

Gabriel, Richard A. "Stress in Battle: Coping on the Spot." *Army*, December 1982, pp. 36–42.

Gal, Reuven. "Unit Morale: Some Observations on Its Israeli Version." Washington, DC: Department of Military Psychiatry, Division of Neuropsychiatry, Walter Reed Army Institute of Research, 1983.

George, Alexander L. *The Chinese Communist Army in Action.* New York: Columbia University Press, 1967.

——————. "Primary Groups, Organization and Military Performance." In *The Study of Leadership.* West Point: USMA Printing Plant, 1973.

Goldhamer, Herbert. *The Soviet Soldier.* New York: Crane, Russak and Co., 1975.

Goldrich, Robert L. "Recruiting, Retention, and Quality in the All-Volunteer Force." Washington, DC: Congressional Research Service, Library of Congress, 1981.

Hammer, Ellen. *Vietnam, Yesterday and Today.* New York: Holt, Rinehart and Winston, 1966.

Harkabi, Y. "Basic Factors in the Arab Collapse." *Orbis*, Fall 1967.

Henderson, Wm. Darryl. "Can-Do NCOs—With Clout—Can Help Cohesion Problem." *Army*, March 1982.

——————. *Why the Vietcong Fought: A Study of Motivation and Control in a Modern Army in Combat.* Westport, Conn.: Greenwood Press, 1979.

Hollander, E.P., and Hunt, R.G., eds. *Current Perspectives in Social Psychology.* New York: Oxford Press, 1963.

Janowitz, Morris, and Little, Roger. *Sociology and the Military Establishment.* New York: Russell Sage Foundation, 1965.

Johns, John H., ed. *Cohesion in the US Military.* Washington, DC: National Defense University Press, 1984.

Jumper, Roy, and Normand, Marjorie Weiner. "Vietnam: The Historical Background." In *Vietnam: History, Documents and Opinion*, ed. Marvin E. Gentleman. New York: Fawcett, 1965.

Kaiser, Robert G. *Russia, The People and the Power*. Brattleboro, Vt.: Book Press, 1976.

Kellett, Anthony. *Combat Motivation: The Behavior of Soldiers in Battle*. Boston: Kluwer, 1982.

Kohn, Hans. *Nationalism, Its Meaning and History*. Rev. ed. Princeton, N.J.: Van Nostrand, 1965.

LaPiere, Richard T. *A Theory of Social Control*. New York: McGraw-Hill, 1954.

Luttwak, Edward, and Horowitz, Dan. *The Israeli Army*. New York: Harper and Row, 1975.

Marshall, S.L.A. *Men Against Fire*. New York: William Morrow, 1947.

Meyer, Herbert E. "The Coming Soviet Ethnic Crisis." *Fortune* 98 (4 August 1978): 169.

Middleton, Drew. "Racial Clashes Said to Hinder Soviet Forces." *New York Times*, 11 July 1982, p. 9.

"More Women Enlist for Soviet Army Duty," *Washington Times*, 28 October 1982.

Moskos, Charles C. "The All-Volunteer Force." In *The Political Education of Soldiers*. Morris Janowitz and Stephen D. Wesbrook, eds. Beverly Hills, Calif.: Sage Publications, 1983.

_____. "The American Combat Soldier in Vietnam." *Journal of Social Issues* 31 (1975): 27. ·

_____. "The American Enlisted Man. New York: Russell Sage, 1970.

_____. "Civil Education and the All-Volunteer Force." A paper presented at the IUS symposium on "Civil Education in the Military," 15–16 October 1981.

_____. "From Institution to Occupation: Trends in Military Organization." A paper presented at the International Congress, Foundation Society and Armed Forces, The Hague, Netherlands, 9–12 May 1982.

_____. "Social Considerations of the All-Volunteer Force." In *Military Service in the United States*. Brent Scowcroft, ed. Englewood Cliffs, N.J.: Prentice-Hall, 1982.

_____. "The Sociology of the All-Volunteer Force." A paper presented at the annual meeting of the American Sociological Association, Toronto, Canada, 24–28 August 1981.

Nyrop, Richard F., ed. *Israel: A Country Study*. Washington, DC: American University, 1979.

Odom, William E. "The Militarization of Soviet Society." *Problems of Communism* 25 (September-October 1976):34–51.

Patchen, Martin. *Black-White Contact in Schools: Its Social and Academic Effects*. West Lafayette, Ind.: Purdue University Press, 1982.

Pike, Douglas. *The Vietcong, the Organization and Techniques*. Cambridge, Mass.: MIT Press, 1966.

Rand Corporation. *Vietnam Interviews*. Santa Monica, Calif.: Rand Corporation, K Series.

Record, Jeffrey. *Sizing Up the Soviet Army*. Washington, DC: Brookings Institution, 1975.

Remarque, Erich M. *All Quiet on the Western Front*. New York: Fawcett-Crest, 1975.

Rochells, Andrew J., and Patton, Paul G. "Demographic Changes in the USSR: Implications for the Soviet Military." Washington, DC: Student paper, National Defense University, 1982.

Rolbant, Samuel. *The Israeli Soldier: Profile of an Army*. Cranbury, N.J.: Thomas Yoseloff, 1970.

Rosenau, James N., and Holsti, Ole R. "US Leadership in a Shrinking World: The Breakdown of Consensus and the Emergence of Conflicting Belief Systems." *World Politics* 35 (April 1983): 368–392.

Scott, Harriet Fast, and Scott, William F. *The Armed Forces of the USSR*. Boulder, Colo.: Westview Press, 1981.

Sharp, U.S.G. and Westmoreland, W.C. *Report on the War in Vietnam*. Washington, DC: Government Printing Office, 1968.

Shelyag, V. V., Glotochkin, A. D., and Platonov, K. K. *Military Psychology: A Soviet View*. Moscow, 1972. Translated and published by the US Air Force.

Shils, Edward A. and Janowitz, Morris. "Cohesion and Disintegration in the Wehrmacht in World War II." *Public Opinion Quarterly* 12(1948): 281.

Smith, Hedrick. *The Russians*. New York: Ballantine Books, 1980.

Stein, Benjamin J. "The Cheerful Ignorance of the Young in LA." *Washington Post*, 3 October 1983, editorial page.

Suvorov, Viktor. *Inside the Soviet Army*. New York: Macmillan, 1982.

Tarasulo, Yitzhak. "The Daily Life of a Soldier in the Modern Soviet Army." A presentation at the National Convention of the Inter-University Seminar on the Armed Forces and Society, Chicago, October 1983.

Taylor, William T., Jr. *Christian Science Monitor*, 17 June 1982, p. 1.

Turley, William S. "The Political Role and Development of the Peoples' Army of Vietnam." Carbondale, Ill.: Southern Illinois University, 1975.

US Embassy. Saigon. *Vietnam Documents and Research Notes*, 1967.

Van Creveld, Martin. *Fighting Power: German and US Army Performance, 1939–1945*. Westport, Conn.: Greenwood Press, 1982.

von Clausewitz, Karl. *On War*. Translated by Michael Howard and Peter Paret. Princeton: Princeton University Press, 1976.

Webb, James. *Fields of Fire*. Englewood Cliffs: Prentice-Hall, 1978.

Webbe, Stephen. "A Soviet Soldier's Lot." *Christian Science Monitor*, Midwest Edition, 3 December 1981, pp. B–24—27, B–30.

Weber, Tom. "Rewarding Things that Count." Washington, DC: Student paper, National Defense University, 1982.

Wimbush, S. Enders, and Alexiev, Alex. *The Ethnic Factor in the Soviet Armed Forces*. Santa Monica, Calif.: Rand Corportion, 1982.

Young,, Warren L. *Minorities and the Military: A Cross-National Study in World Perspective*. Westport, Conn.: Greenwood Press, 1982.

Zasloff, Joseph J. *Political Motivation of the Vietcong: The Political Regroupees*. Santa Monica, Calif.: Rand Corporation, 1968.

APPENDIX

Dollard, John. *Fear in Battle*. New Haven, Conn.: Institute of Human Relations, Yale University, 1943.

Emerson, Rupert. *From Empire to Nation*. Boston: The Beacon Press, 1967.

Etzioni, Amitai. *Complex Organizations*. New York: The Free Press, 1961.

George, Alexander. *The Chinese Communist Army in Action*. New York: Columbia University Press, 1967.

Homans, George C. "The Small Warship." *American Sociological Review*, II, 1946.

Janowitz, Morris, ed. *The New Military's Changing Patterns of Organization*. New York: Russell Sage Foundation, 1964.

_____ and Little, R. *Sociology and the Military Establishment*. New York: Russell Sage Foundation, 1965.

Kohn, Hans. *A History of Nationalism in the East*. London: Routledge, 1932.

Little, Roger W. "Buddy Relations and Combat Performance." In *The New Military: Changing Patterns of Organization*. Edited by M. Janowitz. New York: Russell Sage Foundation, 1964.

Marshall, S. L. A. *Men Against Fire*. New York: William Morrow, 1947.

Molnar, Andrew R. *Human Factors: Considerations of Undergrounds in Insurgencies*. Washington, DC: Special Operations Research Office, American University, 1965.

Moskos, Charles C., Jr. *The American Enlisted Man*. New York: Russell Sage Foundation, 1970.

Shils, Edward A. and Janowitz, M. "Cohesion and Disintegration in the Wehrmacht in World War II." *Public Opinion Quarterly* 12(2), 1948.

Stouffer, Samuel A., et al. *The American Soldier*. Vol. 4. Princeton, N.J.: Princeton University Press, 1949.

INDEX

unit stability in, 47–50
USSR. *See* Soviet Union

Vietcong
  leader casualties in, 129
  legitimate power of, 121
Vietnam. *See also* North Vietnam
  cultural values in, 82, 95–98

Vietnam war, 27–30. *See also* North
  Vietnamese Army
  army strength and, 1
Warfare analysis, 3
Women's role
  in Israeli Army, 73
  in Soviet Army, 72
  in US Army, 71